Slim's Table

SLIM'S TABLE

Race, Respectability, and Masculinity

MITCHELL DUNEIER

The University of Chicago Press • Chicago and London

The University of Chicago Press, Chicago 60637
The University of Chicago Press, Ltd., London
© 1992 by The University of Chicago
All rights reserved. Published 1992
Paperback edition 1994
Printed in the United States of America

01 00 99 98 97 96 95 94   5 4 3

ISBN (cloth): 0-226-17030-6
ISBN (paperback): 0-226-17031-4

Library of Congress Cataloging-in-Publication Data.

Duneier, Mitchell.
    Slim's table: race, respectability, and mascu-
    linity   / Mitchell Duneier.
        p. cm.
    Includes bibliographical references and index.
    1. Afro-American men—Illinois—Chicago—
Attitudes.   2. Afro-American men—Illinois—
Chicago—Psychology.   3. Chicago (Ill.)—Ethnic
relations.   I. Title.
F548.9.N4D86   1992
305.36'896073077311—dc20   91-45637
                                           CIP

For My Father

Contents

PART

1

The Caring Community

1

Slim and Bart

They both came of age at the height of segregation. Sixty-five, a lifelong Chicagoan, Slim is a black mechanic in a back-alley garage in the ghetto. Bart, white, and ten years older, is a retired file clerk who grew up in the rural South. Both are regular patrons of the Valois "See Your Food" cafeteria.

I first met Bart during my early days as a university student, long before I ever set foot inside Valois. Like many older residents of the Hyde Park neighborhood, he ate regularly in the cafeteria of International House, or I-House, as it was called, a dormitory for graduate students close to the University of Chicago campus.

Tall and skeletal in his mid-seventies, Bart dressed in fine suits and sported a Dobbs hat. Sometimes when he'd be sitting alone at one of the cafeteria's long wooden tables, I'd join him and ask about his past. He did not have any strong family ties. His only brother lived in Colorado, and he hadn't seen him in about five years. They spoke on the telephone no more than once a year. He had retired from a long career as a clerk at Swift's, one of the major meat-packing companies, during the era when Chicago was still "hog butcher for the world." Then he took a job as a file clerk at one of Chicago's largest law firms.

Bart moved to Hyde Park in 1928 to attend the University of Chicago as a premedical student and supported himself for a time by working at the Streets of Paris section of the 1933 Century of Progress Exposition. He had little to say about that experience. He had been a ticket collector at the entrance to the shows but had never gone inside to look.

Bart was a very incurious person, one of many odd human beings who become attached to a university community as students and continue the association for decades. His explanation for not marrying was that "some people just never find a person to jive with." His biggest dream had been to become a physician like his father, but the hardships of the Depression made it impossible for him to continue his studies.

He wasn't bitter about his life. The only resentment he ever displayed was toward blacks in the local community. With the southern drawl of the Kentucky town in which he had been raised, he often complained that Hyde Park had long ago turned into a "high-class slum."

Because I thought about Bart only when I saw him sitting in "his" chair after dinner at I-House, many weeks may have gone by before I realized that the old man had been absent for some time. I wondered if he had taken ill. Months passed with no sign of him. I asked the front desk clerk and other residents if they had seen Bart. No one had, and I finally decided that he might have died.

Two years later, when I entered Valois Cafeteria for the first time, I was startled to see Bart sitting by himself eating a bowl of radishes, amidst black men sipping coffee at the surrounding tables. On a chair next to him was the same Dobbs hat I had seen him wearing before he abandoned I-House. He asked me how I had been and inquired about some of the people he remembered from the dormitory cafeteria. He told me that although he had liked being around the students, prices there were high and the quality of food very poor. He had been eating at Valois for a year. I asked what he could tell me about the restaurant, which is known locally by its motto "See Your Food."

"I don't know anything about the place."

"But you eat here every day?"

"Yes, but I don't pay any attention to the place. I just eat my meal and go home."

As our conversation came to a close, he informed me that I might direct my questions about Valois to the owner.

Over the weeks and months that followed, I would see Bart constantly. Despite his claims, he seemed to be well aware of the other habitual patrons of the restaurant, including the group of black regulars that congregated at Slim's table.

I came to learn that Slim's table has, for over a decade, been the meeting place of a group of black men who regularly patronize this cafeteria on the margin of the ghetto. Slim, who comes to the restaurant every day is usually joined by Harold, a self-employed exterminator; Cornelius, a retired meter inspector; Ted, a film developer for *Playboy Magazine* who received an honorable discharge from the army after twenty years of service; and Earl, an administrator at the Chicago Board of Education. These and others constitute a core group that frequents the restaurant daily. Besides them, hundreds of other black men frequent Valois less often, some only on weekends. Ties binding members of the larger collectivity have developed over decades, and it is not uncommon for someone entering the restaurant to be playfully scolded by Slim or his buddies: "Now, don't you go hiding from us again" or "Come by and see us more often," if he has been absent for any significant amount of time.

The spectrum of social classes among the black men is very broad. At one end of the spectrum are a few men like Earl from the Board of Education, middle class and college educated. In the middle, most of the men are solidly working class. At the other end of the spectrum are a significant number who have been downwardly mobile in their later years and have incomes which would place them among the working poor. These are individuals whose wages would place them at or below the poverty line.[1] But even this description is tidier than the reality because most of the men have social characteristics which would place them in various classes at the same time.[2] Most of the men live in small apartments in Hyde Park or local ghettos, but some like Slim own small homes. By the standards of mainstream American society, none of these men are members of the "underclass" or "undeserving poor," though they are sometimes treated as such by whites from the nearby university.

These black men were very much aware of Bart. Sometimes they would refer to him as "the gentleman" because he wore a Dobbs hat and a suit and tie. And then, after another year had passed and they had come to regard his eccentricities with affection, as Bartie. Although Bart seemed to want to remain detached from the blacks around him, he had a neighborly, jocular relationship with them. He found himself inextricably drawn into the social life at Valois as the men began to greet him cordially:

"How you feeling today, Bartie?" Harold once asked him.

"I feel with my hands," was his response.

He continued to sit alone, and the black men came to know him only gradually. Through comments back and forth, from their table to his, they developed a sense for the kind of man he was:

"I bet you got the cleanest kitchen in that building you live in."

"You're right. I don't put nothing on that stove. Not even boiling water."

Interaction between blacks and whites is common on the outskirts of American ghettos.[3] Many American universities are in or close to black neighborhoods, and the territorial margins of these locales are typified by interaction between middle-class whites like Bart and blacks like the regulars at Valois who come from nearby neighborhoods. Whites in such areas often see clusters of single black men routinely passing time together in public places like barbershops, street corners, bars, and restaurants, and blacks who live in these districts have a category in their minds for the "university types" and other gentrifying forces who settle on the margins of their neighborhoods.

Bart was an object of curiosity to many of the men. When he was out of earshot, they would often try to size him up. "Bart's

unusual," Leroy, an electrician, once said. "He is antisocial. He
don't care about nobody. He comes in. He eats. Sometimes he
just sits there and don't say nothin'."

Slim balanced his chin on his thumb and forefinger, trying
not to look in the direction of the old man. "He don't bother
nobody."

After a brief silence Harold glanced at Bart and ended the
sober appraisal. "You ever notice sometimes he fidgets around
when he's eating? He be looking to see if anything is on his tie."

The group of men broke out laughing. "You notice that too?"
Leroy chortled hysterically. "Then he'll take his coat and look
it over to make sure there's nothin' on it." Bart's little quirks
were amusing to the men, but they were also endearing. Later
that night, when he started looking at his coat, the men joked
with him about his ways:

"Bartie, what are you looking for on your coat?"

"Oh, just looking to see if it's okay."

"Bart, you can stop looking at your tie now."

"Oh, I can?"

"Yes, you can."

"Thank you, Harold."

Through such conversations, the men learned very little
about Bart's beliefs and values, but they began to comprehend
something about his temperament. As far as they were concerned, these certain habits and idiosyncracies of Bart's dis-
closed much they needed to know about the old man who sat
near them every day.

Bart had once let it be known that during the fifty years of
his working life he had never been late or missed a day of work.
The only technical exception was on account of a famous crash
of the Illinois Central Railroad. Having been aboard the train
on his way to the office, he once described the devastation for
the men—seats flew out of the train, people were hanging out
of windows, others were lying in the aisles screaming. Bart
somehow remained unscathed. Stepping over bodies, he
picked his way out of the car and got to work a few minutes
late. He seemed proud to let the men know that under the

circumstances, and given his prior work record, the supervisor decided to mark him on time.

"Did you help anybody?" Harold asked.

"No. 'Cause I figured there was nothing I could do, and anyway I didn't want to be late for work."

"Didn't it bother you to just leave like that?"

"Why should it bother me? Wasn't a damn thing I could do. I was on my way to work."

The old man's machinelike routines and indifference became lore among the regulars.

In part, Bart developed a connection to the men through Hughes, a white contractor originally from North Carolina who had a close rapport with several of the black regulars. Like a handful of other white patrons—like the meat-packer Werner Mandlebaum, the landlord Morton Fruchman, and the longtime Hyde Parker Lou Ann Davis—Hughes commanded a great deal of respect. Both blacks and whites in the restaurant thought of him as the finest of men, one who took a deep and abiding interest in others. Like Bart, Hughes was raised in the South, but unlike the older man he was an outgoing, easy-mannered person.

During Bart's first few weeks at Valois, a year before, Hughes had become apprehensive when he saw that the old man walked home alone. He told Bart that anytime he wanted a ride, there was "no problem." For over a year, the regulars at Valois knew that Bart was Hughes's passenger.

At times, Hughes found the old man's inflexible ways to be burdensome and aggravating. Sometimes he would be ready long before Bart, but he would patiently wait for the old man to finish his dinner. Often he would be relieved as Bart took his last bite and seemed to be moving toward the coat rack, only to be disheartened when he realized Bart was actually edging toward the front counter to pick up another bowl of radishes or a dish of vanilla ice cream.

One evening Hughes was expecting an important phone call at his home at exactly 9:00 P.M. He told the old man, who had

long since finished eating, that he had to go. But in a character-
istically rigid manner, Bart said that he wouldn't be ready till
9:30. Hughes had no choice but to leave. The regulars at Valois
feared more for the old man than he feared for himself.

On other occasions Bart would be ready a few minutes before Hughes. His way of hinting that he was ready to leave was
a source of both amusement and annoyance to the regulars.
First he would pick up his hat and coat, bringing them over to
Hughes's table. There he would stand, slowly putting on the
coat, one sleeve at a time, and then the hat. The entire ritual
would last several minutes. Hughes might still be in the middle
of a meal. Although he was tolerant of Bart's ways, he found the
old man's attempts to hurry him annoying.

During one two-week period in the middle of August,
Hughes had to work late. When Slim saw Bart walking home
alone, he was horrified: he knew that the streets around Valois
were dangerous for an old man at night. Bart accepted Slim's
offer of a ride. Slim told Bart that he should never walk home
again, that he would be glad to take him from then on, and Bart
accepted the offer.

Slim is a reserved black man, who has lived near the Hyde
Park neighborhood for most of his life. Slim has an unimposing
but self-assured and dignified presence. He wears the navy
blue uniform of a car mechanic with a zipper jacket that says
his name; a wool cap in winter or a black and white Chevy
"Heartbeat of America" cap in warm weather; and on Sunday,
like many of his contemporaries, Florsheim or Stacy Adams
dress shoes. The Stacy Adams lace up shoes popular among this
generation of men come in two styles, ankle high or low cut.
For the black men, Stacy Adams shoes are to respectability
what a Dobbs hat is for an older white man like Bart.

In his pockets, Slim keeps a chain with many keys (a symbol
of responsibility in the ghetto), and a plastic wallet compli-
ments of the Internal Auto Parts Co. Inside are family pictures,
an Aamco bond card, a driver's license, and an automobile I.D.
He also carries a pack of Camel cigarettes, business cards from

some of the firms he relies on as a mechanic, and loose papers with information related to the various jobs he is engaged in down at the garage.

Slim usually comes to the cafeteria for breakfast and for after-dinner coffee. His back-alley garage off Forty-seventh Street, a ghetto thoroughfare, rented as part of a larger parking establishment, is not visible to pedestrians. But Slim is one of the most respected mechanics on the South Side, and local folks have no trouble finding him. Most of his days, including many weekends, are spent there in the heart of the ghetto. At Valois, Slim is a central figure among the black male patrons, although he is hardly outgoing and rarely demonstrative. To most people who don't know him, he seems aloof and proud. Some people think it is hard to get a fix on him.

The relationship between Slim and Bart intrigued me. Slim seemed to harbor little resentment about injustices of the past, though it was evident from occasional remarks that he had unpleasant dealings with whites once in a while. At the same time, he was a human being with strong moral sensibilities. He viewed himself as a member of a social world characterized by general standards that applied equally to people of all colors.

In the black belt, where traditional family forms are more disorganized than in mainstream society, people often develop substitute kinship ties, in which many of the functions served by families are taken up by other caring individuals.[4] Thus a man such as Slim might take a liking to a senior citizen and do the kinds of things for him that in white society would more normally be done by the man's son, if at all. At Valois, the black counter ladies sometimes even referred to Bart as Slim's "pappy" ("Where's your Pappy tonight?") indicating that in their minds Slim had developed a substitute kinship tie with Bart.

By contrast to Slim's universal morality, Bart was a reserved Southerner who believed that white people were naturally superior to black people. He had not been pleased by the civil rights movement of the 1960s. The fact that he took his meals in the same restaurants as black folks was to him a natural consequence of living in the integrated Hyde Park–Kenwood district.

The two men seldom sat with one another, but at closing time Bart would usually move to a table near Slim's and wait for him to finish his conversation. Bart didn't dare take the firm and resolute Slim for granted as he did Hughes, a fellow white Southerner. He rarely stood up and hinted to the black man that he wanted to leave. He never resisted when Slim told him that it was "time." Usually he would stay by himself until around 9:45, sometimes nodding or even falling asleep at his table. Slim would tap Bart affectionately on the knee to wake him up. The regulars knew that when Slim gave Bart "the tap," the two men would soon be walking out together. Once in a while, Bart would first go to the adjacent liquor store to get himself a pack of Chuckles candy and, on rare occasions, a pack of Camels for Slim.

One November night, some friends and I took Bart with us to dinner at an old German restaurant, the Golden Ox. Werner Mandlebaum, a regular white patron of Valois, had recommended the restaurant to us. As the owner of Chicago's last slaughterhouse, Werner supplied meat to the Golden Ox (as he did to Valois) and vouched for the quality of the steaks. On our way back to Hyde Park from the Golden Ox, Bart asked us to stop by the cafeteria. He explained that he needed to talk to someone for a minute. "My man is still in there, and he'll be wondering where I am." In Bart's vocabulary, there was perhaps no better way to describe the chauffeur that Slim was to him, a man with whom he could occasionally exchange cigarettes for rides.

Given Bart's upbringing and background, there was nothing surprising about his remark. But many months later, the language changed. A young woman who had known him when she was a student came to town for a visit. She later told me that Bart took her to dinner at Valois and said that he had a "friend" in the restaurant, that the friend was a black man, "but"—he emphasized—"he is very nice and he *is* a friend."

The fact that Bart made a point of calling the man his friend, instead of trying to disassociate himself from him in advance, indicated that he had come to value his relationship with Slim. Perhaps Bart was now willing to ignore boundaries that had been vital to him before he grew old and lonely. It seemed also that the very trust he had placed in Slim's reserved but caring behavior had changed Bart's conception of himself vis-à-vis a black person.

I knew that at Christmas time, and for Slim's birthday, Bart would usually ask Hughes to shop for his gifts. Once Bart said to Hughes, "You know what Slim likes. Get him whatever you think he needs 'cause you been to where he works, and I hate to just give him five or ten dollars. The present will show more thought. If you don't mind wrapping the present, I'll get the card."[5]

Though he knew that Bart was trying to show his appreciation, Hughes believed that the old man was being cheap. "Bart, I'm gonna get whatever I think he needs. I'm not gonna insult him by giving him a five or ten dollar pair of socks. Not after what that man's done for you. If you needed that man in the middle of the night, he would be there."

"Well, Hughes, use your own judgment. That's why I want you to do it."

When Hughes picked out a rechargeable flashlight for one of Slim's birthdays and an electric heater on another occasion, it made Bart very happy.

Yet, I sometimes wondered to what extent Bart's use of a more respectful designation, "friend," to describe his relationship with Slim, implied a degree of intimacy. In addition to his feelings of racial superiority, Bart possessed a conception of the male role that militated against vulnerability and closeness with another man, black or white. What kinds of things did these two human beings, raised in a society that earlier in their lifetimes discouraged social interaction between the races, talk about on their way home each night? The answer to my question came more easily than I ever expected it would.

On one of the rare days when I did not go to Valois, I ran into Earl, the middle-class man who was one of the most consistent regulars at Slim's table. On the street near the restaurant, he told me that Slim's old man had died. As all of the regulars knew, many years ago Slim had taken a man in the ghetto "for his father," rather the way he had Bart. In recent months he had been deeply concerned about the older man's health, moving him into a nursing home when he became very ill. Earl told me the details of the death. He had come from the funeral earlier that day, as had some others at the restaurant. Apparently they had all stopped by Valois after the service was over.

When I spoke to Bart the next day, I decided to ask him about what had happened. I hoped that by inquiring into some of the details, I might learn something about the nature of his friendship with Slim.

"What's new, Mitch?" Bart asked.

"Oh, nothing much," I replied. "I ran into Earl and he told me Slim's father died."

"Slim? Yeah. Funeral's tomorrow, I guess."

"Tomorrow?"

"Yeah."

I knew that the funeral had occurred twenty-four hours ago and I took this as a first hint that Bart was not really aware of what had been going on.

"I thought the funeral was yesterday."

"Well, I don't know, Mitch. I just heard that his father died. He didn't mention nothing to me about it, and I didn't say anything to him. A friend of mine gave me the information."

"Who was this?"

"Hughes."

I asked if Hughes had been dressed in a suit the day before. "Yeah, why?"

"Maybe he was coming from the funeral."

"The funeral isn't until tomorrow."

"Are you going to the funeral, Bart?"

"No."

"I see."

After a brief silence, Bart continued, "No, I don't know when the funeral is. Maybe the funeral's tomorrow. I'll be damned if I know."

"Okay, I guess I'll just ask Slim about it when I see him. Did he look like he was depressed tonight?"

"No. Why would he be? He's a grown man. His father was at the age when they all go. It isn't like when you're young. It can happen any time. He lived a long time. You know a lot of them blacks don't live that long. He hadn't been depressed as far as I know. He hasn't been depressed all week. I think his father was in a nursing home for a while. I don't talk to him much about his affairs. I figure if there's something he wants me to know he'll tell me. I don't think he wants me to ask him any questions."

"Well, I don't know. I thought you might have mentioned it to him on the way home one night."

"No, no, no. I don't talk to him about that."

"Did you drive home with him last night?"

"Oh, yes."

"And he seemed okay to you?"

"He seems okay to me all the time. He wasn't any different last night than any other time."

Again there was silence. I decided to try one more time to learn about Bart's private time with Slim.

"I figure that the funeral must have been yesterday, Bart, because I thought Earl said something about that."

"Well now, I may be wrong. I don't say I'm right. I don't know anything about it really. Slim tells me nothing, and I ask him nothing. I figure he figured it's none of my business 'cause if it was any of my business he'd tell me. He don't want me asking him any questions. You know, that's the way I look at it. What he wants you to know he'll tell you, and what he don't want you to know he's not gonna tell you and he don't want you asking."

"Okay, Bart. I'll see you later on tonight."

"Okay, then."

When I entered the cafeteria later that evening, the old man waved me over to his table. He informed me that the funeral had indeed been the day before.

It is evident that the relationship between Slim and Bart is not one of great depth. Yet Slim places a value on Bart that goes beyond the occasional exchange of a pack of cigarettes or a Christmas gift for a car ride home. Slim often tells me he doesn't think it right that people neglect their elders. His attitude of caring exists within a framework of barriers to closeness set up by Bart, perhaps to protect himself from developing too much intimacy with a black man, or simply with any man.

The standards by which Slim treats Bart are universal, applying equally to any elderly person, black or white, in or out of the ghetto. Inside this restaurant on the margins of the ghetto the black regulars have entered into an affirmative relationship with the wider society, orienting themselves to situations that make it possible for them to apply their high standards and adopting unique social forms, like the substitute kinship tie, beyond the fringes of the black districts.

One day Bart collapsed inside the restaurant and was rushed by ambulance to the University of Chicago hospital. As it turned out, he was merely dehydrated, and within a day he was back at Valois on his usual schedule. Many of the regulars asked about his health, and on one occasion Leroy, the electrician, began telling him what he should do, how much water he should drink, and which foods he should eat. After a few minutes, Bart responded in his typically direct manner: "I appreciate your concern. But it's none of your business and please change the subject."

Leroy responded, "Bart, it's because I love you and I think a lot of you. That's why I'm saying these things. . ."

But Bart wasn't pleased. "Well, thank you for your concern, Leroy. But I can manage pretty well." And that was that.

Others asked Bart about his health, too. As Hughes explained to me, "It was a constant thing, because people don't have anything to talk to Bart about. I have to dig to the bottom of everything to find anything to talk to him about."

So Bart was annoyed.

A few weeks after he first collapsed in the restaurant, he began to feel dizzy again. This time he was at home, and he telephoned Hughes. The men agreed to meet at the hospital later on that day. When they arrived, Bart decided to check in for tests, and he told Hughes that nobody in the restaurant was to know he was there: "Don't say nothing to anybody in the shop about it. I hate for everybody to see me and say, 'Oh, how are you feeling? Oh, I hear you're sick.'"

Hughes recalled the conversation he had with the old man. Bart was tired of being asked about his health, all right. With a smile he concluded, "So don't tell anybody, Hughes. If anybody asks me about it, I'll know you told them."

"Don't you think we should tell Slim?" Hughes responded.

"What do you think?" Bart asked.

"Well, Bart, think about it . . ."

"Well . . ."

"Bart, Slim's your friend. And you know all the things we do for each other. And if Slim finds out somehow that you been in the hospital when you wasn't at Valois and didn't let him know. . . . You owe it to Slim to let him know."

"Well, you're right. I hadn't thought of it that way."

The two men tried to figure out what Hughes would tell the others at Valois.

Bart came up with the solution. "Just tell them that in this cold weather I'm eating in a restaurant closer to home until the weather breaks."

Hughes said, "Bart, that's real good. That way we don't have to get into details or anything. I can tell them and be so casual and change the subject so fast that they won't have any reason to come back with another question."

After he left the hospital, Hughes stopped by Valois to tell Slim the news. The instant Hughes walked in, Slim asked, "What have you done with my daddy?" Hughes sat down and explained what had happened.

Slim said, "He probably never should have been sent home the last time."

Hughes explained, "He was getting rid of more liquid than

he was taking in, and through evaporation and everything, that can kill you. Even a severe diarrhea can dehydrate you. Everything's checked out okay other than that. All he needs is the right blood pressure medicine and to drink his fluids."

Slim said, "Well, he's like a machine. He has a glass of orange juice in the morning at home. Then he walks six blocks to the restaurant and has two cups of coffee. And then a little later he has a glass of water. Then at night he has two cups of coffee and a cup of tea."

With a laugh Hughes added, "And that's it. And if they tell him to add three glasses of water, he'll add three glasses."

Both men had ambivalent feelings about Bart, some positive and some not. It was not uncommon for sentimentality and humor to mingle when they talked of him. As they sat together at the table, Hughes told Slim more about what had happened at the hospital:

"I took him a couple of candy bars. I went over to the liquor store because I know he always goes in there before you drive him home. I described Bart to the guy behind the counter. He said, 'Oh, yes.' I said to him, 'What kind of candy does he buy?' He laughed, 'Chuckles.'

"So I took a couple of Chuckles to him. When I walked into the hospital room, he said, 'What do you got?'

"I said, 'Chuckles.'

"He said, 'Hughes, I don't eat candy. I don't eat candy.'

Slim and Hughes laughed together.

"I said, 'Well, they're here. And if you get hungry you can have them.'

"He said, 'Well, why don't you take them with you and eat them?'

"As I reached for them, he put his hand in the air and said, 'Leave one.' I don't know if he didn't know how to . . . all he had to do was say thanks.

"Then later on I said, 'Bart, would you like a cup of coffee or something.' He was a bit chilly.

"So I went down to the restaurant, and it was like a maze in that hospital. I've gotten well acquainted with most people who work there because there's hardly an employee there I haven't asked for directions! When I finally reached the cafeteria, I figured I'd get him some toast to go along with the coffee. Sometimes he tells me he eats a cookie or something before he goes to bed.

"So I finally found my way back to his room. I said, 'Bart, here's the coffee.'

"He said, 'Well, put it down. I'll only have two sips of it anyway.'

"And two sips is what he took."

"He said, 'Hughes, you finish it. And I wish you wouldn't get me anything more than I ask you for. I don't want any toast.' I said, 'No problem, Bart.' I wanted to say, 'Stick it up your ass!' But I said, 'Bart, it's better to have it and not want it than to want it and not have it.'"

Slim and Hughes laughed. Together they had gone through so much with the old man that they understood each other's feelings exactly. As Hughes later described it, "Oh, last night I could have chopped him up into little pieces and today I like him." Hughes told Slim how he had felt earlier that day when he went to Bart's apartment to pick up the things Bart had asked for at the hospital:

"As soon as I walked into his apartment his real pretty overcoat, the real nice one, was over a chair. And right next to it on the table was his Dobbs hat. When I saw him again later on I said, 'Bart, everything in your apartment was okay. But one thing really upset me. When I saw your hat. I know the complete history of the hat. And the hat is you up and down. And when I saw your hat and realized where you were, and not knowing just what the outcome would be, I really had a few seconds of feeling sad at that moment. 'Cause I thought ahead and I said, "Oh my God. That poor hat!"'"

Again, Slim and Hughes laughed hard. Then, before he went away, Hughes went over the official story with Slim, emphasizing that not a soul was to know Bart was in the hospital.

At the restaurant that night, before I'd heard anything about the conversation between Slim and Hughes, I sat with Harold,

Earl, and Slim. It was very slow. We were about the only ones present, and it was one of those evenings when it seemed that nobody had anything to say. The biggest event was when a Greek accent would yell, "Cheeseburger's ready!" and the men would look to make sure someone had risen to pick it up from the counter.

Suddenly I turned around to check where Bart was and found that he was nowhere to be seen. Turning to Slim, I asked about the old man. He responded that Bart was having his meals at home until the cold weather let up. Later, as the workers cleaned the steam table in preparation for closing, Spring and Ruby, the counter ladies, yelled across the room to Slim: "Where's your Pappy tonight?"

Slim repeated what he had just told me. Harold asked Slim if Bart was okay and Slim said, "Yes."

I thought nothing of this incident until later on that evening. On my way home from the restaurant I stopped by Bart's apartment to see if there was anything he needed in the freezing weather. I rang his bell for five minutes and got no answer. When I arrived home, I attempted to reach him by phone and again received no answer. It occurred to me that Bart might have gone back to the hospital. I called the switchboard and asked whether Bart was listed. He was. When I finally reached Hughes the next day and told him I had spoken to Bart, he explained why Slim hadn't told the truth. Before we hung up, Hughes said, "Whatever you do, don't let Slim know you know. Because he might think I told you."

As I reflected on the previous evening, I was struck that Hughes conceived of himself as living up to standards which were not his alone but were also embodied in the moral authority of Slim. Although middle-class blacks are usually conceptualized as potential role models for other blacks, here an exceptionally sensitive middle-class white man sought the respect of a working-class black man as he attempted to live in accordance with high ideals.

I marveled at the willpower and self-control that Slim exhibited on a night when nobody seemed to have anything to say.

After all, the whole circle could have gotten a lot of mileage out of that news. Despite his complicated feelings for the old man, he demonstrated a tremendous respect for Bart's privacy. Slim's perception of his own moral worth could not be separated from a disposition to act in accordance with standards appropriate to his associates, whose worthiness was taken for granted in that setting. A person of the weak moral constitution portrayed in major accounts of the black male would have preferred to let his friends know that he was on the inside.[6] At Valois, Slim and his sitting buddies demonstrate an inner strength characterized by self-control and willpower that is seldom, if ever, attributed to the black male in social scientific and journalistic reports. Though black men are usually portrayed as so consumed with maintaining a cool pose that they are unable to "let their guard down and show affection,"[7] these black men had created a caring community in which one of the men, Leroy, had even expressed his feelings for Bart by telling him the men were interested in his illness because they loved him.

In Thomas and Znaniecki's *The Polish Peasant in Europe and America*, one of the first great field studies in American sociology, the authors emphasized that immigrants to America not only were transformed by the society of which they became a part, but had a transforming effect on that society as well.[8] The same can be said about the relations between blacks and a wider, integrated society, though we more commonly focus on the welfare rolls, the murder rate, and the prison population in understanding the way that blacks, and especially black males, have changed America. Here, on the margins of the ghetto, I witnessed the adaptation of one of the ghetto's prevalent social forms, the substitute kinship tie, to show, through little acts of caring, an alternative conception of civility and of what it means to be a black man.

Bart died alone in his studio. When, one Tuesday evening, he didn't show up at the cafeteria, Slim notified Hughes, who called the manager of Bart's building.

"The manager just called me back," Hughes told Slim an hour later. "He had opened the door, but the chain was on it. He is waiting for the police to come. I can't say a thing about it, but it doesn't look good."

Slim suggested that Hughes call Bart's brother in Colorado. "They haven't spoken in a year, and he'll want to know."

Hughes got the number from directory assistance, reached the brother, and reported back to Slim: "I just tried to tell him that Bart might be in trouble. But he cut me off, saying, 'He isn't nothing but a bachelor. Who's gonna miss him?'"

"That's a horrible thing to say," said Slim. "How could a man say that about his own brother?"

"I told him we were waiting for the police to enter the room," said Hughes. "That I would call him back when we knew. But he told me he takes his phone off the hook when he goes to sleep. I said, 'Don't take it off tonight. That way if he's gone we can get hold of you.'"

Bart was found dead at the side of his bed, one leg in his pajamas, one leg out.

Hughes dialed Bart's brother, but the line was busy. The building manager referred the Chicago police to Hughes for the brother's number, and an officer called Colorado himself. A few minutes later he called Hughes back to report the constant busy signal. "That's all you're gonna get," Hughes told him.

Bart stayed in the city morgue three weeks. Hughes says he died the way he lived. "We all die alone, but he died totally alone, being in the morgue for so long." In truth Bart wasn't completely by himself. He had Slim, and he had Hughes, and he had the entire caring community at Valois.

Bart did not have to be intimate with Slim to feel affection for him. The moral authority embodied in Slim's caring behavior had pushed Bart to the limits of his own potential for tolerance, friendship, and respect.

Yet, the power of integration over ingrained beliefs is slow and incremental and should not be exaggerated. Years later I asked Hughes, who had himself so clearly looked up to the black man, whether he believed that Bart had changed as a consequence of his relationship with Slim. "There was only so much he could change. But it certainly made him more accepting. He saw what it means to care for another person. It gave him an understanding about the caring behavior of the black race. He probably figured at least some could be human."

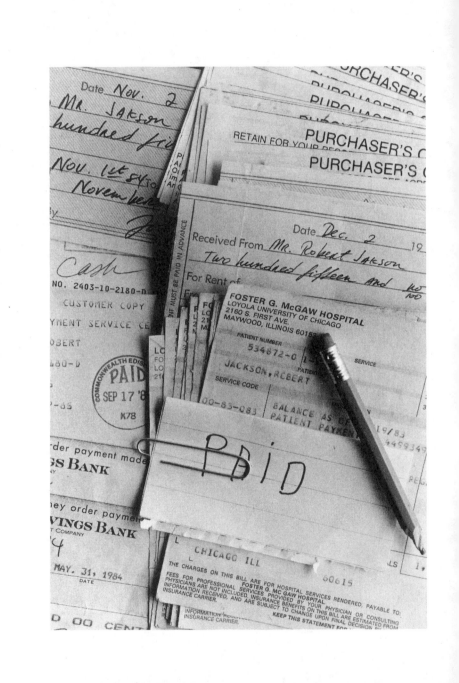

CHAPTER

2

Black Men:
Transcending Roles and Images

Perhaps no statistic is more troubling and has had a more hor-
rifying effect on images of black men than that derived from a
widely reported private study indicating that 609,690 black
men in their twenties are "under the control of the criminal
justice system—in prison, in jail, or on probation or parole"—
23 percent of black men in that age group.[1] Although the study
specifically included men on parole and probation, when the
exact same statistic was discovered in New York State, the *New
York Times* headline read, "One in 4 Young Black Men Is in
Custody, a Study Says."[2]

Black men are badly misunderstood, probably no less because of the well-meaning liberal media's constant barrage of
images showing how bad things have become than to Republican advertisements indicating that liberals have placed killers
like Willie Horton back on the streets. But the statistics as they
are reported paint a depressing picture no matter what spin
you put on them. The life expectancy for black males is 66
years, while for white males it is 72.3 years. The homicide rate
among black men is six to seven times higher than the rate
among white men; they are most likely to be killed by other
black men. Forty-five percent of black males are likely to become victims of violent crime three or four times in their lifetime. In 1988, cerebrovascular disease caused 57.8 deaths per
100,000 black male population, compared to 30 per 100,000 for

white men. The divorce rate among black men is the highest of any group. These statistics tell us most of what we know about what it means to be a black man in America,[3] but they tell far too little about the black man's inner strength—his resolve, his pride, and his sincerity.

Slim and his sitting buddies possess self-esteem, which they regard as justifiable to the extent that their behavior accords with specific notions of moral worth. When they conduct themselves in a way that causes them or others to believe they have failed to live up to those standards, they are embarrassed. When they are treated by others in a way that is inconsistent with their self-esteem, they sometimes feel the mental anguish that is associated with injured pride.

My relationship with Jackson, a semiretired crane operator and longshoreman, is typical of many friendships that taught me about the prideful natures and resolve of these men. Jackson was in his middle sixties when we met. We had become quite friendly during my first year in the cafeteria, talking on a fairly regular basis. When I moved to an apartment on Fifty-first Street, I discovered that Jackson had been living in the same building for ten years. Although we rarely visited each other's studio apartments, Jackson occasionally invited me in to show me personal papers or photographs. Like many ghetto dwellers, he didn't have a checking account or a telephone. He gave my number to his attorney when he needed to be reached. We often spoke about the common problems we faced with our landlord, about our respective families, about my experience growing up on Long Island, New York, and his experience as a migrant from Mississippi to Chicago.

Jackson was easily embarrassed by the men who often passed the time near our building. Once he was standing outside when the daughter of a man he knew and respected walked by. The men on the corner had been addressing every women who passed, and she was no exception. Jackson had kept himself separate from the men, so as not to be associated with their

conduct. But when his friend's daughter passed, he felt morti-
fied: he worried that she would think he had put the men up to
making their remarks. I learned about this incident when I
heard some of the corner men talking about it: "He don't say
nothing to women unless they be leaning his way—way, way
over," one man said in an attempt to show how timid Jackson
was. "He told me, 'You know I'm not going to jail for no woman.
Because in jail I can't get nothin'. I might have to give some
up.'"

When I saw Jackson at Valois a few days later, I asked him
what the men outside were talking about. He said, "Those men
stand out there and meddle with every young thing that passes.
They meddle with them women. They say everything. The
girls keep walking. They don't stop. Most of them ignore the
remarks. It makes me feel embarrassed, and they know it.
Especially when they talked to my friend's daughter over
there. It really hurt. Because I've been over to her home to
see her daddy and I've tipped my hat to her mamma. I apolo-
gized to her the next time she went by. She said, 'Jackson, I
know you didn't.'" It hurt Jackson's pride to be associated with
actions that testified to standards below his level of moral
worth.

Jackson's problems with the landlord were the basis of many
of our discussions. Our studios were in a terrible state of disre-
pair. The first time I went over to Jackson's place was when,
knowing I had a camera, he asked if I would take photographs
of his apartment so that he could use them as evidence if he
ever decided to sue. Paint was chipping and peeling on all four
walls and flaking down from the ceiling. The stove didn't work.
The wall beneath his window hadn't been properly insulated.
The bathroom light socket had come out of its fixture and dan-
gled on a wire a few feet above the bathtub.

Two years passed before a new stove was installed. And it
took another nine months before the building's manager
decided to do anything about the condition of the apartment. During that period, the landlord left an old form letter
in Jackson's mailbox:

Dear Tenant Mr. Jackson:

In addition to the country's problems of the energy crisis, we also have the problems of rising cost in electricity bills, heating bills, real estate taxes, scavenger service, plumbing, insurance, maintenance of the building, and almost every other product imaginable.

Because of all this we must like everyone else, in order to stay in business, pass some of the rising costs on to you. Starting July 1st the monthly rent for your apartment number 201 will be $205.

My records show that you have no security deposit. Your monthly rent is $205. You must make up the difference and bring your deposit to equal your rent. Please make arrangements with manager.

If my records are not the same as yours regarding security deposit, then bring receipt or cancelled check as proof.

Thank you for your cooperation.

At the bottom of the page, there was a handwritten request: "Please have this paper signed and return it to me as soon as possible."

Unlike newer ones, the long-time residents of the building had not been asked for deposits when they moved in. Jackson was offended by the request, the tone of the letter, and especially by the message at the bottom. He had paid his rent promptly for ten years. He ignored the note and never heard another word about it.

A few months later the landlord appeared at Jackson's door.

"What do you want done to this place?" the bulky landlord asked.

Jackson glowered. "Nothing."

The next morning we saw one another at Valois and he began to tell me that story. I was in a rush, and I asked if we could continue the discussion in his apartment that evening. When I stopped by, he pointed out all the repairs that needed to be done, and began his story all over again.

I said, "But Jackson, why didn't you simply show the land-lord like you just showed me? The landlord wouldn't have come by if he wasn't going to fix it."

He replied, "I couldn't do anything but just look at him." Staring up at the ceiling, he continued, "Look up there. Now what would I want done to this place? Now why would he have to ask me a silly-ass question like that?" It would have been an indignity for Jackson to begin detailing the problems when they were so obvious. His pride was so great, his resolve not to be made the fool so powerful, that he had reacted by simply clos-ing his door on the landlord.

In the same conversation he complained to me about the manager's request for a security deposit. That incident had also injured his feelings; he was a man who took pride in paying all his bills. In order to demonstrate how seriously he took his obligations, he told me the story of the invoice he received after he had incurred great expenses for being hospitalized with fluid in his lung.

"I'll show you the bill."

He pulled a cigar box off his shelf and took out an itemized invoice that amounted to almost three thousand dollars.

"Look at the whole thing," he said as I shuffled through the papers. "Man, I was fucked up! I was there thirty-nine hours before they took that fluid off."

Then, with pride and satisfaction, he showed me the pay-ment receipts.

"I paid every goddam dime of it. I paid it. I could have run away and not paid it. 'Cause they didn't know shit about me."

As he showed me each receipt, he continued talking with a mixture of personal satisfaction and contempt for the landlord. "No matter how the landlord treats me, here's something for me to feel good about inside. Here's the last receipt I paid that hospital. And then I sent them a thank you card. I could have run off on them. They didn't know where I was or nothing. See? But this landlord treats me like a goddamn dog. I paid that hospital every goddamn nickel. Of course I paid. That doc-tor saved my life, man. But anyone else would have showed them a ghost. I been here ten years and never missed my rent. You can tell a crook because he trusts no one. I have paid my rent on the first of the month every time."

In the three years that I knew Jackson, I had never heard him boast or brag, and this conversation was no exception. He found the landlord's approach degrading. His satisfaction in fulfilling an obligation was not self-aggrandizement, a boastful attempt to raise his own position in another's eyes.

Like many of the regulars at Valois, Jackson has convictions about the proper behavior for a man of his kind and about the minimal standards he will tolerate in behavior directed toward him.

For persons characterized by such pride, every act of participation in the wider society calls for an appropriate bearing. Some men, like Slim and Jackson, are proficient in conducting themselves in such a way that their demeanor is an outward manifestation of their "respectable" self-images. The deportment of other men, possessed of similar high standards, may fail, in others' perception, to communicate their notion of their moral worth, and they may therefore be treated in a way that is inconsistent with their own self-assessment.

Take the case of Willie, well known at Valois as "the man in the pink suit," whose outlandish garments include shirts fastened with Hefty Bag wires in lieu of buttons. Willie and I met after I had been coming to Valois for a few weeks. He was the first person in the restaurant to make friendly overtures toward me. Leaning over from another table, he asked, "Young man, do you know what the word 'inevitable' means?" It was obvious to Willie that I was one of those "university types" the black regulars would so often describe as I came to know them in the years to come.

"It means that it has to happen," I responded.

"I say, you be up on your book learning, young man."

In the months that followed, Willie was very nice to me. On long nights in his roach-infested room at the Hyde Park Arms

Hotel, we would often look through his own copy of Webster's dictionary and talk about various words that interested him. Willie often said that although I seemed to have book learning, I didn't have enough "street intelligence" to get by in the world: "When we're through with our lessons, Mitchie, you'll have both street intelligence and book learning on your side."

Willie made his way in the world by trying not to take things at face value. He told me he'd let the Greeks at Valois know he was watching them, to ensure they'd give him good cuts of meat. He was suspicious that certain pot pies, filled with less chicken, were set aside for people like him. He often inspected his slices of pumpkin pie to make certain they were the same size as those given to other patrons. The man in the pink suit lived with the constant expectation that the institutions of society—from chicken shacks to cafeterias to banks to government agencies—would take advantage of him if he didn't look out. This world view was not unlike that of many black regulars at Valois, and indeed he shared in their desire to adhere to standards of moral worthiness. But in ways that made him unusual among the black men, his demeanor caused others to treat him in a way that failed to accord with the image he had of his own value.

Unlike most of the black regulars who felt it improper to sit for too long in the cafeteria, the man in the pink suit often sat for hours at times when it was clear the Greeks needed their tables. Often he was boisterous. He was one of a very few men at Valois whose outer-directed, attention-seeking, self-aggrandizing behavior actually did conform with sociology's typical portrait of the black male. With jokes and stories he made constant claim on the attention of those around him. Sometimes he would go on for long periods in a loud voice that entertained the men at neighboring tables while disconcerting occasional customers who didn't know what to make of the scene. Finally, he was asked to leave. To this man, whose life largely centered around one small cafeteria, the inability to comport himself in accordance with the requirements of that setting was a crushing blow.

Willie was not banished. At a crowded moment Spiro, the owner, simply asked him to give up his seat. But Willie's pride was badly hurt. He had been coming to Valois twice a day for seven years. It just didn't seem right to him that he should have been singled out. The old man told the regulars that he wasn't being treated like a man and that he would not return.

Willie had come to view himself as a central figure at Valois. He was someone who, people said, was "given to illusions" after a stroke, but who received the attention he sought anyway. At one time he had been associated with some important boxers, and he often went down to the gym to give rubdowns to the fighters. Before his stroke he had performed as a musician, but these days he said that he couldn't "do the fingers anymore." With a pink suit and a loud voice, he often embarrassed the men whose attention he sought, men who did not want to be associated with his flamboyant ways. And yet those same people often took delight in Willie—in his jokes and in his manner. Unlike them, he was not sufficiently attuned to his environment to control his behavior in the presence of families or students who came to the cafeteria. Yet, he had at least always made a purchase.

It was a cold November night when the old man was asked to leave the crowded restaurant. Spiro had to choose someone. He singled out Willie because the old man had long since finished his meal and because Willie had been noisy. Spiro intended no harm. He needed the space. Thinking he could depend on a regular like Willie to understand, he said, "Why don't you take a walk and come back a little later?" Instead, Willie returned to his little room at the Hyde Park Arms Hotel feeling devastated and enraged. He had always known he wasn't "in with them Greeks," but he also believed that most of the action at that restaurant centered around him. The men who laughed at his jokes, the patrons who gaped at him from afar—all of this had made him feel that he was the life of the cafeteria. The man in the pink suit decided that he would go somewhere else from then on, and he firmly believed that the crowd from Valois would follow. After all, as he later told me, he had been the first to bring all the best jokes and stories to the cafeteria.

So he started eating his meals at Wendy's. When, through the fast-food restaurant's big window, I first caught a glimpse of him there, he was waving a knife at some young black kids who had been making fun of him from another table. "They don't show no respect for older people," he told me when I walked in. "They're saying to themselves: 'It's the first of the month—check's comin' in. Let's follow that sucker. Hit him in the head and take his money.'"

The week before, he confided, a group of kids had followed him out of Wendy's and surrounded him. He was frightened. One ruffian threw a can. Another asked for money. They started making fun of the Hefty Bag wires he was using in place of buttons on his shirt. He kept resisting the voice inside that urged him to show the pistol he always carried. "What will they pull on me?" he wondered. Finally, he whipped it out for them to see. Some of the kids were scared and started running, threatening to notify the police that he had a gun. Limping along as fast as he could, he made his way to his hotel—up in the elevator, all the way to the end of the hall, where a skeleton key, after some fiddling, would open room 320. He stashed the gun.

Back out on the street all was calm. The cops appeared. When they saw that it was the man in the pink suit, smiles lit up on their faces. They knew he was harmless and he knew they knew it. The old man brandished a wrench. "Hey man, I don't know why they told you this was a gun."

Wendy's had a much younger clientele, and Willie was clearly unhappy with the environment, though he often talked up its hamburgers and apple dumplings in an effort to rally Valois regulars to eat there. He would often tell his friends that "they don't charge you for no second cup of coffee. You got to watch that."

But to his surprise the old audience was not about to change its hangout for him. Sometimes individual members of the group who pitied him would come to Wendy's for a few minutes to "shoot the shit." But these visits were relatively short. He learned the hard way that the black regulars were more attached to each other and the cafeteria than they were to him. When people urged him to return to Valois, his eyes would light up momentarily. But he would respond firmly, "When I tell you good night that don't mean good morning!"

Possessed of markedly less self-esteem than his associates, Willie was vain. Desiring constant attention and approval, he never stopped trying to entertain and impress those around him. Yet, although less autonomous than the others, he too conceived of himself as a man committed to a mode of life embodying a conception of moral worth, and his mental anguish was not unlike that experienced by all of the black regulars when they were treated in a manner that did not accord with their self-conceptions. Once he explained himself to me more fully:

"Don't go to any one place too often or they think you don't have any other place to go. I go to a lot of different places now. I like to spread my money around. I am a man just like you are a man. I can go anywhere I want. But a man does not go to places where he is not appreciated."

If we take seriously the lessons of contemporary sociology, men like Willie with distorted needs for approval, recognition, and material possessions constitute the model for ghetto-specific masculinity. To be sure, such individuals are common in poor black neighborhoods, but Willie lived in a constant search for a mixture of attention and affirmation that most of the other black men took for granted in the cafeteria setting.

For the black regulars, passing time at Valois consists of participating in the same rhythm of various routinized episodes that yield both companionship and solitude. These repetitive sequences are significant because they guarantee the recurrent presence of close acquaintances while establishing them as people who have "things to do." The routines of most of the men therefore demonstrate full awareness of the times when they might be in the way at the cafeteria. Rather than put themselves in the position of spending too much time in one place, they make a point of developing routines that show a certain independence of the establishment. No matter how gratifying collective life can be, excessive time spent in one place can demean a man. This is why routines also function to guard the individual against a likely challenge to his pride. Self-respecting people cannot help experiencing a certain amount of embarrassment when they appear to others to have nothing to do and no place to go. As Luther, a newsstand attendant, says: "A man without things to do is not a man."

Clearly defined personal activities and repetitive processes are constituents of both individual autonomy and collective solidarity. Collective life among the black regulars is therefore characterized by intermittence and recurrence. The same people are usually present at similar times each day or week. But gatherings do not necessarily occur among them with that same regularity. Collective life does not consist of a continuous flow of interaction among all the members. It is, rather, a now-and-then phenomenon that occurs with some unpredictability, in varying arrangements, from day to day. A few habitués routinely sit alone at separate tables and only join members of the larger collectivity on rare occasions; many choose to sit by themselves at least sometimes. Most participate in a variety of subgroups drawn from the wider collectivity of black men. It is not uncommon for individuals to begin by sitting with a small group, later to change partners or move to another table by themselves. Often men who gather at one table will engage in constant conversation; at other times those same men will sit quietly with one another or simply make occasional comments while reading their newspapers in each other's presence. The average length of these gatherings is about forty-five minutes but it is not unusual for men to sit together for twice that length of time.

Some of the black cafeteria regulars are retired, others still work. Hanging out, not unlike traditional forms of work,[4] is organized around specific bundles of tasks that need to be accomplished if only to satisfy obligations to oneself. The example of Drake is illustrative. He is a retired butcher who brings lottery tickets to the Greek owners every night in exchange for reimbursement and a cup of tea with lemon. He sometimes works as a substitute at the newsstand on the same block as the restaurant. Seven days a week he travels on the bus from his nursing home, eight blocks away in the ghetto, to Fifty-third Street. Men like Drake create satisfactions for themselves by establishing, in their times of leisure, conditions not unlike those of their former jobs.

Drake's day is organized into tasks. At 10:30 A.M., when he goes to Wendy's to have a cup of coffee and read his morning paper, he is engaging in the first important event of the day. After sitting for three-quarters of an hour, he stretches, glances at the clock, looks around the restaurant, and then goes back to his newspaper. At 11:30 he gets up and goes next door to Valois. What is the significance of Drake's moving from one restaurant to another at the same time every day? The answer might be found in a particular aspect of the world of work which molded him. Most regularly employed people discover that within a job boredom can be minimized by changing the form of activity from time to time.[5] Drake's routine consists of different activities that make the day more interesting than it would be if he were to spend all of his time in one place.

Once he is inside the cafeteria, Drake sits down to talk with his buddies for a few minutes. He comments on the news of the day and makes predictions about future baseball or football games. He says hello and shakes hands with the men he regularly sees. Having checked in, Drake walks up to the front counter where he joshes with the Greeks and orders his usual. When he sits down, he always goes alone to the same table. He sits with his newspaper for at least forty-five minutes. At Wendy's he read the sports section; at Valois he reads the business section. He reads the paper in the same order every day. After he finishes reading, he looks at the clock and shows signs of restlessness, stretching and turning his head. Soon he rises, orders a refill of tea, and joins friends at another table. He is likely to stay with these same people until he leaves the cafeteria at 1:00 P.M.

What is the significance of the various activities this man has built into the time he spends at any one place? It would be simpler merely to observe that Drake goes to Wendy's at a certain time and moves along to the cafeteria. But as just one part of his day illustrates, each event consists of a variety of separate activities. The man who spends his life on a regular job learns to conceive of work as a series of self-contained tasks. This is not the same, of course, as changing the form of activity when Drake moves from Wendy's to Valois. Conceiving of the period spent in one place as a series of self-contained activities keeps a long stretch of time in the same place from seeming interminable.

Hanging out consists of discovering types of activity that result in predictable and desired amounts of companionship, conviviality, and solitude, and the ability to bring about new experiences by changing the conditions within each type of activity. Contrasts and choices among the alternatives are made manifest after men have been inside the cafeteria for an extended period of time. It is common for them to alter the conditions of passing time by joining new people at other tables or even by moving away from a group to sit alone for a period of time. The social world is large enough—especially when the cafeteria is crowded—to ensure that each man can sit with many others without ever getting tired of their company. It is through such processes that men with time on their hands avoid boredom.

There are middle-class people in the Hyde Park neighborhood who view the black men at Valois as bums and loafers. But the men involved—like Drake—experience their days as productive. They have been molded by the ideals and necessities of the conditions of their work. The black regulars seem to be temperamentally suited to establishing routines that provide maximum satisfaction[6] from simply keeping busy, engaging in a range of repetitious activities from day to day. This enables them to preserve their self-esteem and to feel they are taking part in chosen activities, rather than residual ones, and this in turn helps them to feel that their own lives are meaningful.

Although the men often congregate at the same table, it is not unusual for them to settle in separately, without even acknowledging the presence of those with whom they sat only a day or a meal earlier. Normally they mingle with the same general group of sitting buddies, but not always. Sometimes the same men might sit together no more than once every few weeks. But regardless of the extent to which collective life is intermittent, individuals do tend to be present on the same schedules each day. There is always a balance between copresence and intermittence.

Few of these men are disposed to elicit constant affirmation from their friends and acquaintances. Often, many weeks can pass between the interactions of two people who have warm feelings for one another. In such a context, the "insult" plays an important role in communication. A harmonious relationship is often acknowledged and affirmed through the use of rough words. Here Johnson walked into the restaurant and noticed Claude, whom he had not seen for a while.

"Hey you little fat-faced fucker, where have you been?"

Happy to see his friend, Claude replied joyously, "Dirty bum! You senile old man! When the hell are you going to retire?"

Playful insults of this kind have a role in the now-and-then structure of interaction at Valois.[7] They enable regulars who have not seen one another for a period of time to reaffirm the warmth that existed the last time they were together. Boldness and effrontery serve to remind men that although time has passed, each still has a place in the others' hearts. These ritual indications are symbolic of the stability of relationships, assuring men even as autonomous as these that their importance to others inside the cafeteria is by no means precarious from encounter to encounter.

Regardless of the extent to which collective life takes on a now-and-then character, such rhythmic sequences bring about the recurrent presence of the same group of others in a man's life. Although interaction is frequently interrupted, the routines of those involved are nevertheless important to the group. They are the vehicle by which the black men can depend upon the recurrent presence of specific others in their lives.

If a man is asked why he hangs out with the same people at the same times throughout the year, he may say, as one man did to me, that it is just happenstance or he may deny the existence of repetitive sequences altogether, so as not to imply that he is a creature of habit. But if some do not recognize or admit to their own routines, they are the exception rather than the rule. In fact, the very significance of routines to collective life is sometimes a topic of discussion among the men themselves. Most of them are capable of describing in general terms the sequences they see from day to day. They also show specific awareness of the time patterns of each of their companions. The image of collective life in the minds of group members is partly a function of each man's awareness of the routines of his associates. The sense that one is a member of a collective life is served by knowledge that he participates in a common repetitive process.

A man places a value on his own recurrent patterns and on those of his friends as well. This is the case not only for those with whom he sits frequently but also for persons he encounters at more unpredictable intervals. Comments and questions like "You're late tonight" or "Why have you been late the last few nights?" or "Where have you been? We were worried about you!" are heard over and over again. Whether explicitly stated or not, one reason many men come to the cafeteria at particular times is that they are expected—and they expect others to be there as well. As Leroy says, "Sometimes when I'm tired I know I should come down to Valois because everybody else be coming. People expect to see you. It's part of the day." Particular routines are a vehicle by which both self-respect and companionship with the same people are maintained. The expectation of regular participation in collective life is one of the greatest single sources of support a man can find—short of a wife and children.

Although they are occasionally intolerant of middle-class blacks or university students, the black regulars usually grant unconditional acceptance to other members of their own group, treating one another with respect and socializing with discretion. These poor and solidly working-class black men are notably different from the prevailing stereotypes about them. Despite the contradictory ways in which they are treated by their society, they are consistently directed by standards within themselves.

Though the black regulars sometimes use humor to embarrass their associates in a good-natured way, they do not usually attempt to humiliate them or put them in their place. For them, the disposition to be frank about their own personal weaknesses rather than to create fictions which might serve to increase others' sense of their worth is proper behavior. These remarks about Slim, intended to explain why he is popular, emphasize the significance of sincerity to group members. Harold says: "As far as Slim goes, I like his honesty. Slim sits up there and tells me about people, about what is happening to him. And he is honest about it. He won't cover up what's happened to him. Slim will come around and tell it like it is. He'll say, 'Look, I don't mind giving her all the money, but she shouldn't mistreat me.' That's the way it is. It's Slim's honesty that I like."

Ozzie echoes Harold's view. "I'm closer to Slim because he's very honest. Slim tells me what he does to women and how they treat him, which is unfortunately sometimes the opposite of the way he treats them. That's honesty because some men don't say that. Slim will not always tell you that he is in the dominating position. That he got the best of the deal. He'd say, 'Man, you know I gave her fifty dollars. You know she told me she wouldn't give me that money back.'"

A willingness to disclose personal weaknesses is not unique to Slim. Most of the black men have opened up in some significant way. This is most evident in discussions about personal life, where rather than viewing themselves as lovers and exploiters, men often commiserate as victims. In discussing the

Oscar nominations that the film *The Color Purple* received, for example, Harold said he had no interest in seeing another movie that "slandered" the black male. Black men are often portrayed as exploiters and users of women, and the regulars are acutely aware of this. Elliot Liebow's description of some lower-class street-corner men is not untypical of the stereotype they attempt to live down. He writes, "But more often, [they] prefer to see themselves as the exploiters, the women as the exploited, as in assessing a woman's desirability in terms of her wealth or earning power or in equating being 'nice' with having a job. . . . The men are eager to present themselves as exploiters to women as well as to men. . . . Men saw themselves as users of women as sex objects as well as objects of income."[8] The black regulars are sensitive about such images because they know that the society they live in, from its best sociologists to its funniest comedians, associates them with similar stereotypes. These are not men who pass the time speaking of their conquests; more often their daily conversations focus on what they regard as their own vulnerability. Rather than presenting themselves as lovers and exploiters, they are straightforward about their weaknesses and their inability to dominate the opposite sex. They often speak of difficulties they have in finding the right women. Rather than being in the dominating position, many are anguished by their inability to meet women who share their ideas and values.

Ozzie's story about his affair with a woman suggests the kind of personal feelings regulars sometimes relate to one another. Often such stories detail the difficulty a man has in dominating the opposite sex. The story also illustrates the clash in values that sometimes occurs between black cafeteria men and the women they meet.

Ozzie began by saying that he could be too sentimental at times.

> I look at the sky and I look at the birds. I'll feel sentimental if it's a balmy day or something like that.
> I met a girl at the newsstand. I was sitting there talking

to the paper man and this nice looking girl walked by and said hello to me.

I asked her how she was doing and she started telling me about some guy. What he did to her. She said her ribs were cracked. She was standing there in pain. I said, "How long has this been going on and why did you let him do this?"

So we went and sat down over by the bench where the bus stop is and talked about things in general, and she started telling me about him and then about men, about how they always want to rush her to bed.

So when I heard this that tells me something right away. What is she looking for? After all, I'm a bachelor. She started telling me how men bother her along the streets. So I thought, "Well, maybe she wants me to say something to her."

So we were talking and then I said, "Are you doing anything right now?" And she said "No." So I said, "Why don't we go to the Tiki bar and have some beers?" She said, "Okay." This was about eight o'clock. So we go across the street and she grabs my arm like we're old friends. I didn't say nothing. I've had that happen before.

We gets into Tiki and I order a beer and she orders some fancy drink. That's the way most women are. They be drinking beer until you come. Then they order an expensive drink. A high-class drink.

So she drank it, and she said, "What do you do?" I said, "I'm a case worker. I work in public aid." She said, "Are you going steady with some girl?" I said, "No, I just date." So that told her right there. I'm on the make. So everything was fine.

Then I get to see this girl maybe two or three times a week. And she starts coming by uninvited and all this kind of stuff. Nice intelligent girl. Speaks very well. Comes from a very good background. Her daddy works and her mamma works. Very intelligent.

But it so happened that she wanted to be a gypsy. You

can come from a good family and still want to be a bum. She wanted to roam free and rebel against the rigid guidelines she was brought up with.

We had a lot of fun. She was easy to get along with. But I noticed that at different times she would come to visit me, she would have different attitudes. She had no marks on her legs or arms from drugs, but I couldn't help but notice that her moods would change. She would say, "Hey, do you have a joint?"

Then one day she asked me if I have cocaine. I said, "I don't smoke reefers and I don't use cocaine. Not that I'm a square. I used to drink alcohol regularly, but I decided to stop except for occasions. You like coke?"

She said, "Yeah. I like it once in a while." So I knew that I was in trouble. And I also noticed that walking along the street with this girl, all the men knew her. All the young men knew her. All the middle-aged men knew her. All the old men knew her. That's a very bad sign. Very bad. With all this AIDS going around I immediately goes on alert. I also noticed that after sex she didn't like to wash up too much. I didn't like that. You see what I'm trying to say?

So I said, "Look lady, we're going to have to part company. I live in a different world than that cocaine world." I told her that I didn't like the way she took care of herself. She had five children with five different men. She would become fascinated with some guy and latch onto him until she became fascinated with somebody else. I tried to tell her she was on the wrong path. I tried to give her the experience that I've had. She can use it. But you can't make people do nothing if they don't want to do it. I have a habit of trying to change people, but they can't change if they don't want to change.

Such is the frustration of working men whose values clash with the women they encounter. Although many of the black cafeteria men believe they have been victimized, this does not imply that they do not themselves try to dominate a relationship. The truth, often acknowledged in discussions about tactics, is that such a goal is not easily attained. On one very typical autumn evening, for example, Billy Black, a repairman for the Chicago Transit Authority, in his late fifties, Harold, the exterminator, and Earl, the retired Board of Education administrator, were talking:

"People fight all the time," Black said.

"It's the only way to iron out your disagreements," Harold responded.

"I never mistreated my wife once in all the years we was married," Black said.

"I think now, Black, after all my bad experiences, that I've come to believe in the things that the cave man did," said Harold. "Men have to be tough-skinned."

I asked Harold what he meant.

Laughing, he responded, "You white folks are apologetic and intelligent with women. But that is the problem the white man has with women. And black folks have trouble then they try to be like white folks in this way. Women like to think they are needed but that you have taken control of them. They don't want an understanding like 'He's gonna be nice to me in this way and I'm gonna be nice to him in that way.' Emotions don't run like that. Through all his education, the white man has dulled his edges. When it comes to woman and man relationships, white people have a tendency to be too damn intellectual. Now that is not one of the true prerequisites of making love. It's the emotion, the passion. You don't have time to ask a woman what kind of degree she has. You see what I'm saying?"

Before I could respond, Black cried out, "But we is not savage, Mitch. Hit my wife? Never. When we would have a fight, I would just lock the bedroom door, lock all the windows down, and then go to sleep."

The men laughed, as if to indicate that they understood from experience.

Black said, "We got in an argument one time and I went to

walk out the door. And she just laid down in front of the door. Told me I wasn't going anywhere. I cooled down. But I never hit her."

I asked, "Does she live in your neighborhood now?"

"If she lived near me, I'd move even further away. I look at her face and can't believe I was married to her for fifteen years."

Although Harold and Black have different ideas about the best way to treat a woman, they share a readiness to acknowledge that they have been victims rather than exploiters. Naturally, such discussions place the blame on the women rather than on the narrators. But implicit in their attitude is a recognition of how difficult it can be to remain dominant, even for those who have successfully maintained that crucial nexus between work and masculinity. And often a man's words to his friends might both place blame on the opposite sex and explicitly admit weaknesses and shortcomings, as Leroy's comment demonstrates: "I had a bad experience in my marriage. After my wife started working I couldn't relate to her because I didn't have as much education as her. She'd go gambling with her girlfriends. She'd go off on a Friday and I wouldn't see her till Sunday. I couldn't cope with it. So I told her I wanted a divorce."

The disposition to be honest rather than to create fictions that might serve to prop up others' sense of one's own value is the true achievement of worth in the eyes of their associates. These are not men who find it necessary to show others what "kinda studs"[9] they are. By living in accordance with principles such as pride, civility, sincerity, and discretion, these men confirm for themselves—rather than proving to others—that they possess some of the most important human virtues. Thus they make evident the extraordinary strength of their sense of self and their ease with their own selves. In each of these qualities one recognizes a different aspect of the fixed conception of self-worth that inheres in these men. Quiet satisfaction, pride, inner strength, and a genuine expressiveness without effusiveness here coalesce in a type of masculinity that is certainly more widespread in reality than in current accounts of the black male in the mass media and in sociology. Slim and his sitting buddies have created a caring community that crosses boundaries of race. The men transcend the usual limits of the male role. They are vulnerable and expressive while living with resolve and remaining directed by standards within themselves.

PART

2

The Moral Community

3

Valois as a "Black Metropolis"

Walk the Streets of the Black Belt and you will find no difference in language to mark its peoples off from others in the city. Only the black and brown and olive and tan faces of Negro Americans seem to distinguish it from any other section of Midwest Metropolis. But beneath the surface are patterns of life and thought, attitudes and customs, which make Black Metropolis a unique and distinctive city within a city. Understand Chicago's Black Belt and you will understand the black belt of a dozen large American cities. (Drake and Cayton, *Black Metropolis*, 1945)

No section of any American city has been examined so thoroughly as those districts of the South Side of Chicago portrayed around the Second World War in Drake and Cayton's landmark book, *Black Metropolis*.[1] Though the South Side ghettos are not as typical as many would like to believe, so many political and cultural movements have begun there and so many of the nation's black leaders have resided there that this district is often called the capital of black America.[2] It is the largest contiguous black district in the country in the most segregated city in America. Despite these factors, which probably make black life there atypical,[3] the emphasis on Chicago in so many important American books about blacks is mainly due to the great influence of the Sociology Department of the University of Chicago. From the pioneering work of E. Franklin Frazier's studies of black family life and class structure to the detailed community study embodied in Drake and Cayton's *Black Metropolis,* to the more recent ecological studies of Gerald Suttles and William Julius Wilson, the department has amassed an extraordinary number of facts and theories about ghetto life in its city.[4] Even the novelist Richard Wright acknowledged the influence of this academic movement in forming the image of blacks in his classic novels *Native Son* and *Black Boy,* and his famous character Bigger Thomas:

> I did not know what my story was, and it was not until I stumbled upon science that I discovered some of the meanings of the environment that battered and taunted me. . . . The huge mountains of fact piled up by the Department of Sociology at the University of Chicago gave me the first concrete vision of the forces that molded the urban Negro's body and soul. (I was never a student at the University. . . .)
>
> It was from the scientific findings of men like the late Robert E. Park, Robert Redfield, and Louis Wirth (all of the Chicago sociology department) that I drew the meanings for my documentary book, *12,000,000 Black Voices;* for my novel *Native Son;* it was from their scientific facts that I absorbed some of the quota of inspiration necessary for me to write *Uncle Tom's Children* and *Black Boy.* *Black Metropolis,* Drake and Cayton's scientific statement about the urban Negro, pictures the environment out of which the Bigger Thomases of our nation come.[5]

Perhaps because such a large number of the major works on American blacks have been based on reporting in Chicago, the neighborhoods that constitute the South Side have come to embody the stereotypical American ghetto, despite their extremes of segregation and size.

In the middle of this large set of neighborhoods, surrounded by them on its three land sides, is the integrated Hyde Park community where, on Fifty-third Street, Valois Cafeteria sits.

Best known as the site of the University of Chicago, Hyde Park
is also the sometime residence of many black public figures and
personalities such as the Reverend Jesse Jackson, Minister
Louis Farrakhan, Muhammad Ali, and the late Harold Washington, Chicago's first black mayor. Just west of Lake Michigan,
Hyde Park lies six miles southeast of Chicago's business center.
It is an historic area whose black and white residents are accustomed to social contrasts—contrasts between fine homes and
"section eight" low-income housing; between some of the best
academic bookstores in the world (including the Seminary Co-
operative Bookstore and Powell's Books) and branches of the
best chicken and rib shacks of the near South Side (including
Harold's Chicken Shacks 14a and 14b and Ribs & Bibs); between the BMWs of Chicago's "buppies" (black urban professionals) and the maroon-striped campus buses that transport
thousands of white students through streets considered to be
dangerous. Indeed, surrounded on three sides by black slums,
Hyde Park has an ambiguous reputation for safety. Some long-
time residents, black and white, regard the area as secure; it is
patrolled by both city and campus police. Most, including
many university students and staff, fear and avoid areas just a
few blocks away from the campus. This is especially true at
night, when streets like Fifty-third Street turn into another
ghetto thoroughfare, populated by many more blacks than
whites. Hundreds of teenagers from the surrounding black belt
will often do their socializing on the street near Valois on Friday
and Saturday evenings, attracted to the neighborhood by the
movies of the Hyde Park Theatre.

Valois Cafeteria, known locally by its motto "See Your Food,"[6]
is the heart and pulse of Hyde Park.[7] Its sixty-year history at
three neighborhood locations is well known, especially to some
of the older white men, like the little dentist and horse player
Dr. Amsterdam and the late court buff Jim Clark, who went
downtown to the Loop daily to watch trials in the federal building from the day he retired to almost the day he died. Patrons

said the cafeteria and the action in the courtroom downtown kept him alive. He lived in the local East End Park Hotel for three decades before he passed away and held court on anything that happened in the Hyde Park–Kenwood neighborhood. By the time I met him, he had lost most of his eyesight, but his memories were quite vivid.

"Valois has been in Hyde Park since the early twenties. William Valois opened his first restaurant two blocks from here. . . . [8] He called it 'Valoys,' because that's what the populace called him. He was a French Canadian and I'm sure it was pronounced 'Valwa,' but he and everybody else just called it 'Valoys.' He had the restaurant there until the time he died, and then his son unloaded it. He sold it to a man named Walter Allman."

Allman's widow, long remarried, still lives in Hyde Park. She sold the restaurant to Greeks from the same village as the current owners, Spiro and Gus. Since then, twenty-five years ago, she hasn't been able to bring herself to go back. On a hot summer day we sat in her apartment just a few blocks from the restaurant:

When I married my first husband, Walter Allman, he used to drive around Hyde Park, and we'd drive on Lake Park Avenue and he'd show me this awful-looking hole in the wall. "If I ever owned a restaurant, that's the one I'd want to own." He knew that it drew people from all over the city, that every walk of life was represented. When he told me that was what he wanted, I just couldn't believe it. But eventually he bought it.

After he had it for six years, urban renewal came along, and his customers demanded that he relocate nearby. My husband was the owner when it moved to its present location. In order to relocate, he had to pay over a hundred thousand dollars, almost three times what he paid the Valois family for the original restaurant.

It immediately proved very worthwhile. When my husband died in 1969, they were serving twelve hundred customers a day. He didn't try to make a lot of changes in the operation because he never wanted to spoil a good thing. People would come great distances for baked beans, stew, chicken pot pie with big chunks of chicken.

There was one doctor who had a great big dog. This doctor ate at home, even though he didn't like his wife's cooking. But he came in every night for a piece of beef or a hamburger because there was no place else, including his home, that had food good enough for his dog.

One woman was a big Chicago philanthropist. She lived in the same hotel as Jim Clark. She used to come in with a big shopping bag full of papers. The rumor in the restaurant was that she carried all of her stocks and bonds around with her.

I used to go and sit there trying to get my husband to come home early. There were about four customers who came in every day and wanted angel food cake. So every blessed day I made that angel food cake. That's how my husband was. He was a perfectionist. I'm sure that nobody in this city gets better food than that.

The same people ate there every night. There were tables of unattached white men. Either widowers or never married. They would look at every customer coming in, and it was like a family.

Mr. Allman's widow recalled that each person had his own "social clan":

I used to be so amused when I would come in and sit at the front table. Because I am a born people-watcher. If I could have written, boy could I have written a book! Some of these things were so funny. And every person was an authority on something, usually on the most irrelevant material. And what they conversed about each day! There was no great brilliance that would knock you over, but this was a very important part of their life. It was a home to them.

It was a cafeteria and anyone could sit where they

wanted to. But these regulars were upset if some outsider dared to sit at their table. At three o'clock in the afternoon, it was mostly the women. There were many women—widows who lived in the hotels around. I think they had little kitchenettes. But they couldn't get food like that and they knew a good deal when they saw one. At noon it was largely men.

The clientele was largely white. I can recall no blacks at first. It got more and more so. But it was never a majority, like I hear it is now.

Today the Greek owners estimate that twelve hundred daily patrons still come from both the immediate neighborhood and the surrounding black ghettos. In addition to retired men and widows, there are white and black office workers, construction men, executives from local businesses, police officers, university students, and merchants from the block. Overall, most of the patrons at Valois are black, but at particular times of the week, especially during the lunch hour, a vast majority of them are white. During the restaurant's off-hours, when men can sit for long periods without taking up needed space, blacks outnumber whites. The neighborhood, which was 3 percent black in 1950, had reached 47 percent by 1990.[9]

Many of the single black men, and some of the single white men, rent rooms with kitchenettes. Their small apartments have space for no more than a couch where they sit or lie when reading the newspaper, watching television, or falling into a doze. Often there is scarcely any separation between a man's living space and his sleeping space. When he sits alone inside the house or apartment for too long, the silence and isolation bother him. He explains why he keeps television or radio on in the background: "I can't stay nowhere when it's like a graveyard." In neighborhoods with living quarters of this type, people need the kind of collective which the cafeteria provides. Sebastian Hardy, a retired white telegraph operator, estimates that three-quarters of the people who come to Valois are from such neighborhoods: "They live in sleeping rooms. They don't have kitchen facilities. I got a nice kitchen in my apartment, but I come in here because I know a lot of people in here. And it doesn't cost much more to eat in here than to cook at home. In the winter, on a night when it's too cold or too windy, maybe I stay home and do my own cooking. But over here in this neighborhood it's sleeping rooms. People in the Hyde Park Arms Hotel, they can't cook. They have a hot plate or something. They don't want to cook. They don't want to bother. They can't carry groceries home from the store. They are alone in those little rooms. They want out."

In many cases, those who gather at Valois each day find that making their own meals—grocery shopping, cooking, and washing dishes—is too demanding, especially given the psychic cost of having meals alone. As Cecil, a black divorcé and retired IRS agent, tells me, "It's just not worth it to spend hours in the supermarket, hours making the food, and then cleaning it up when you're gonna sit alone at the table eating the meal."

And Claude, a police officer, says, "Some people might be saying that they come for the food. That this is the only place around to get a good baked chicken. But I admit that I don't favor the solitude at home. I was spoiled while my wife and me was together. We would eat at home. Alone I can cook a good meal for myself, but I favor to be with people when I eat. These men are like my family now. Because we eat together every day."

Many other regulars, black and white, have previously been married and used to stay with their families in the evenings. They began showing up at Valois after bereavement or a broken heart brought loneliness and, sometimes, desperation. About these things they do not often speak. Instead, talking about current events, or human quirks, or the geography of the city, or daily problems, they try to put the bad experiences behind them. "That's water over the dam," they tell each other. "And you can't bring it back." Finding themselves alone in the Hyde Park neighborhood or surrounding ghettos, they seek companionship, most often during mealtimes, when a man is especially inclined to desire company.

At one point a number of articles about Valois were published in local newspapers, and the mostly blind Jim Clark took note:

It used to be that you could sit there and enjoy the food and have it digested before you leave the building. They've got too much publicity now. Us fellows who sit in the park go in at 4:30 now to beat the rush. With my eyes, as bad as they are, I couldn't read the article in the Chicago *Reader.* But I looked at it with my magnifying glass. It would say continued on page twenty-eight. There were three columns. Then I turned the page again. Two columns. Then I turned it again. One column. Well, people read that stuff. And most of the people who read it are liberals anyhow. They don't have any animosity toward black people, so they will come out to Hyde Park from the North Side to eat. Guys ask me about it downtown when I watch the trials in the courthouse. "That cafeteria in Hyde Park must be a good spot to eat?" "Yeah," I say. "They do a terrific business."

Allman carried on the restaurant in exactly the same way Valois did. In fact, he kept Wilson, this colored fellow who had worked for Valois. In those days there was no blacks allowed to eat in the restaurant. He worked in the back. The only time we'd see his arms was when he passed the food through the opening.

The younger colored people are not used to patronizing this type of place. They eat junk food. But you still have this type of old-time colored people that appreciate it. So you've got 80 percent colored customers. Where else are decent colored people gonna find this kind of food? They like the potpie and the short ribs, and they like the safe atmosphere here in Hyde Park.

Jim Clark's stereotypical observations and anachronistic designations aside, there is no doubt that these men have recreated elements of the old Black Metropolis that once flourished with greater intensity there. Indeed, there is a great perception among the black men themselves that the public life of the old ghetto described by Drake and Cayton has declined, the restaurants and barbershops of those districts having gone the way of the rest of the black belt. The quantitative demographic studies that would confirm these perceptions are conflicting, but ethnographic data suggest that many of the establishments that remain are heterogeneous places where men who regard themselves as upstanding have to mix with hoodlums and winos.[10] Some of the black regulars are themselves prone to claim that those folks who remain at the old hangouts are somehow lacking in dignity. As Ted says, "Those who don't think like us, they stay in the ghetto and never venture out." Some upstanding men like the regulars feel out of place in such company. Regardless of the extent to which the ghetto has been transformed, there is no doubt that these men are acting in accordance with the belief that it has.

The process by which they share in the traditions of the old neighborhood at Valois begins with the reproduction of those forms of dignified, intimate, face-to-face contact that once pervaded the social world of the ghetto—its residential areas, its old main streets, its barbershops and cafeterias. Small-town stuff has always facilitated intimate contact among these black men, and the old world itself lives on through face-to-face contact. It lives on through the conservation of what Robert Park once called the "extraordinary zest for life," an exuberance in the conduct of everyday affairs that is a habit of the mind.[11] It lives on in their patience, in their quiet dignity, in their ease of manner, in their sense of humor.[12] It lives on in memories and beliefs, the vitality of which are conserved through processes of interaction in the new hangout.

There are, to begin with, those ineffable, yet predominant, qualities of the old ghetto that were once taken for granted but that can no longer be assumed. These are aspects of life that

57

serve to fortify certain fundamental conceptions that members of the group have of themselves, qualities of life with a significance that has no logical foundation and that can ultimately only be felt in their bones by those who know the sensations well. If it is impossible to transplant to Valois the particular sounds, smells, and sights of the old neighborhood, at least here the black regulars can enjoy the kind of solid food in good company that brings back images of a world that once existed for them just a few blocks away. Valois is not a soul food restaurant; it is not one of those places where men can find smothered chicken, candied yams, beans, greens, and cornbread any more than they can find the broken sidewalks, alleyways, and gutters of the old main streets. But these days, just the fact that an inexpensive meal is prepared the old-fashioned way, with natural ingredients on a stove or in an oven, satisfies the longing of men who dread fast food and microwave styles of food preparation. As Earl says, "At Valois they cook. You can watch them cook. If you look in the kitchen you know they are cooking there. The oven is full of stuff, the stove top's full of stuff. I'm not exactly in love with efficiency. Us older folks don't care about that. Never mind how efficient it is. What does it taste like when you finish it?" Comments such as "Mamma cooked from basics" and "Mamma never used packaged stuff" are typical of a generation of black men who feel very much at home in a cafeteria that offers its patrons a kind of food that is symbolic of the integrity of their older way of life.

The restaurant also facilitates participation in the old neighborhood through the role it plays as a central meeting place. It is a notable constituent of masculinity in the ghetto to pass time with one's peers in a regular hangout, and male clusters have always been an important dimension of the public life of the ghetto. At Valois, men who want to "shoot the stuff" or see their friends in a "jumping" or "popping" hangout feel at home. As Officer Wilkens suggests,

> Lots of people—even though they don't live in the neighborhood—make a point of coming to Valois to eat.

It's sort of like a meeting place. You suddenly run into someone you haven't seen for a while. "Oh, there's Horace. I haven't seen Horace in years." Valois has been here for a long time. So you have a group of people that's been coming here for a long, long time. I can come here and— like yesterday—I saw one of my buddies who I haven't seen in a while. He returned a year ago. But he comes back. In fact, I saw two other people I know, who I haven't seen in a couple of years. People come back again hoping to see people they haven't seen for a long time.

Such comments are evocative of the old Chicago ghetto's main streets and parks described decades earlier by Drake and Cayton in *Black Metropolis*. The old neighborhood had many central meeting places that served a function not unlike that of Valois:

> Black Metropolis has a saying, "If you're trying to find a certain Negro in Chicago, stand on the corner of Forty-seventh and South Park long enough and you're bound to see him." There is continuous and colorful movement here—shoppers streaming in and out of stores; insurance agents turning in their collections at a funeral parlor; club reporters rushing into a newspaper office with their social notes. . . . This is . . . [the area's] central shopping district. . . . As important as any of [the major community institutions] is the large four-square-mile green, Washington Park—playground of the South Side. Here in the summer thousands of Negroes of all ages congregate to play softball and tennis, to swim, or just lounge around.[13]

The black men have memories of life in Chicago that are not simply nostalgic fantasies. The cafeteria takes on greater significance because it is a meeting place that encourages the kind of sociability found in the old Black Metropolis. Many regulars no longer feel sufficiently comfortable to engage in such interaction inside the ghetto. As Ted said, "We used to go out running early in the morning. And you could see people who had slept out there all night. Not bums. These people had brought their little barbecue thing. And they would just stay, because in the good weather it was wonderful to be outside. It was families. Wife, husband, kids. Or just people. They'd sleep there. Don't you try to do that now."

With the deterioration of larger meeting places, some men who regard themselves as decent, upstanding, and moral choose a place where they can participate in the kind of interaction that they say once prevailed in a more concentrated way elsewhere. A restaurant like Valois cannot possibly have the enormous significance of the old Forty-seventh and South Park described by Drake and Cayton. But socially even this small cafeteria, at particular times of the week, has an intensity and a vitality that can make a man like Ted look back on an earlier period: "Sometimes it reminds me of the olden days when it used to be at the barbershop where everybody hung out. Especially on Saturday morning when it's main gas day. I think back to the barbershops and to the Powers cafeterias. That's when you did your main gassing, on Saturday morning. And at Valois everyone makes sure he gets there on Saturday. I always make it on Saturday. There's gonna be six or eight guys at a table for four and everybody's shifting around and everybody's there."

Of significance, too, is the neighborly quality of interaction that men find at the cafeteria, a style they associate with the old Black Metropolis. They lament the absence in their lives of the kind of encounters that were common in that old community.

One day Leroy came over to my apartment. Some of the men knew that I had moved and had helped me do some of the work, like laying down the carpet, installing a fan, and putting up bookshelves. This was the first time Leroy had been over. It was a hot August day and we each had a can of beer. As we sat there he asked, "How many people in your building do you know?"

I told him that I knew only a few other residents.

"In the old days you would know everybody. You would have

been inside everybody's apartment. Because in the old days people would have come around with little offerings when you first got here. Pies. Cakes. They would have come in. They would have the cake. You have the coffee. 'I live in so and so.' In a year's time you would have dropped into everybody's apartment."

On another occasion a few black regulars at the table next to mine began reminiscing about the intimacy that had long since disappeared from neighborhoods in which they lived.

Ted began: "On our block you would get chastised by any old lady. 'Boy, what are you doing over here? Does your mother know you are over here?' She'd get you on your toes by the ear and she'd drag you home. 'I found him over on Lafayette.' You could get chastised by anyone in the neighborhood."

"That's true," Slim said. "Oh, yeah. You had about twelve mothers, seventeen fathers. Everybody knew what you did."

Ted continued, "We would be out on the corner. All the police would say is, 'I want this corner. I'll be back in five minutes.' If you weren't off the corner, they'd throw you up against the wall and go through this ritual. And your neighbor would come by and see this and say, 'Ted, what did you do?' 'Nothing, ma'am.' That would not be believed."

"Yeah," Slim said, "you got looked out for in that old neighborhood."

Ted went on, "When you came home late, you would see curtains parting. Oh, sure. You could be on your own front porch at 9:00 P.M. The neighbors would say, 'Don't you think it's time for you to go on in?' Your father would get out of work and the neighbors would see to it that you ate. Oh, that was a neighborhood."

Part of what makes the cafeteria a warm and cherished place for these men is the manner in which convivial life there conjures up memories of a community now partly dispersed from its original territory. Yet such an interpretation should not lead to the stereotype that all moral persons, or even all of these men, have left the ghetto. The spectrum of engagement and disengagement from the ghetto is actually quite wide in its empirical reality. On one end are men who reside, work, and socialize in the ghetto. Somewhat further over are those who work downtown but have their residential and convivial life at places in the ghetto. Toward the other are men like Slim, who still live and work in the ghetto and usually have one of their daily meals there, coming to a restaurant on the margins like Valois for additional conviviality. At the other end of the spectrum are men like Ted, who moved to Hyde Park after he retired from the army, takes the bus to work downtown, and eats his meals either downtown or at a Hyde Park restaurant like Valois.

The men at Slim's table represent a steady mixture of these alternatives. In years gone by, they passed most of their leisure time in restaurants that lined the ghetto main streets.[14] They reminisce about the old Powers cafeterias in which they sat endlessly—talking, laughing, and watching the people go by. In the barbershops, they would huddle in the back of a small room or on the stoop, listening to the "dusties" on a radio or playing checkers or pinochle. They would tell jokes and stories and carry on serious discussions about politics, religion, and society. These were important meeting places, playing a role in helping them develop and preserve ways of looking at the world that were drawn from their experiences. Such institutions still exist in the ghetto, but Valois fosters the kind of interaction these particular men seek there less frequently. The integrated cafeteria concentrates a remnant of another world in a new, relatively stable hangout.

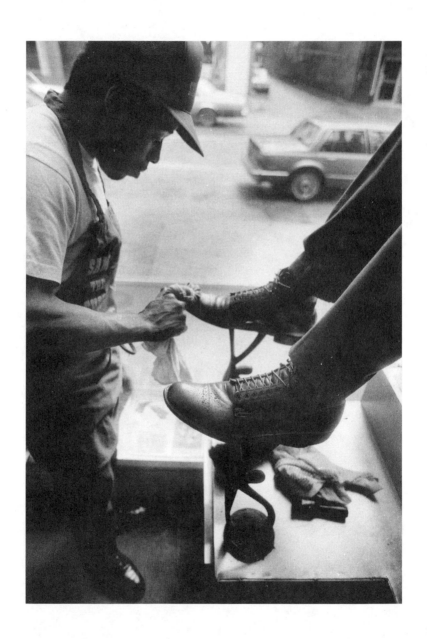

CHAPTER

4

The Standard of Respectability

Slim and his sitting buddies want to live in accordance with notions of appropriate or correct behavior. The idea of "respectability"—defined as a mode of life conforming to and embodying notions of moral worth—has great significance for them. They are people with definite opinions about the kinds of conduct appropriate to their level of moral worth and of the minimal standards they are willing to tolerate in their own behavior or that directed toward them.

The black regulars are members of an age group that together witnessed the deterioration of nearby black areas. The oldest, like Drake, a retired butcher, and Bond, an insurance salesman, were born around 1905; the youngest, like Ted and Harold, around 1935. They range in age from their early fifties to their early eighties. Within this group there are obviously smaller age divisions. Yet the men conceive of themselves in similar ways, as individuals who have lived contemporaneously.

Their conceptions of decent behavior are pervaded by nostalgia and cynicism. They associate moral worth with the patterns of behavior that predominated in the ghettos of their childhood. They long for an earlier time, especially within the black community, when their own virtues were treated with greater respect by other blacks.

The regulars demonstrate impatience with those who do not share their memories and disdain for those who do not attribute validity to them. They place great value upon experience as a source of knowledge. Their views are most often legitimated by memories unique to their age group. Their nostalgia cannot be separated from a concomitant disposition to regard the wisdom that derives from their experience as among the most valid forms of knowledge. Through references to the quality of their own judgment and morals, and an ardent generationalism, they especially differentiate themselves from both middle-class and younger impoverished blacks, many of whom can be seen in the local Hyde Park neighborhood.

If respectability can be defined by the sociologist as a mode of life embodying conceptions of moral worth, it is defined rather more loosely in actual practice by a man's opposition to a number of human characteristics he disdains: wastefulness, pretension, aggressiveness, uncommunicativeness, impatience, flashiness, laziness, disrespect for elders, and perhaps most important a lack of personal responsibility—all of which are taken by Slim and his sitting buddies to be features of a social disorganization that has ruined the ghettos of their youth. This pattern of values is "unrespectable": It is beneath the level of moral worth that they associate with their own existence.

On any given day, at any given table, it is possible to hear the widest range of views articulated by the black regulars. When an outsider is present, the range of views may narrow. This is especially true in conversations about racial issues, where some men are more reluctant than others to hang what they perceive to be dirty laundry in public.

What are the particulars of the general standard of respectability? What kinds of attitudes do these men have toward the external world? Like most working-class people, the majority of respectable blacks live with a conception of the correct relationship between means and ends that is often expressed in evaluations of the proper relationship between exertion and reward. During the prosperity of the 1980s, the "correct" order of these relations underwent great distortion in both the ghetto and the wider society. The effect of young urban professionals on the one hand and drug dealers on the other was to insult the common-sense understanding of this proper order for men who are almost ascetic, quietly satisfied with their humble lives.

Their attitude toward middle-class blacks is therefore tinged with an outrage characteristic of the moral sensibility the better-off blacks offend. They criticize them for their wastefulness and attempts to be sophisticated. The black regulars cannot understand why the middle-class blacks prefer to take their meals at more expensive and seemingly pretentious places like nearby Mellow Yellow or Orly's. On one occasion, Wilkens, a light-skinned policeman whose father had been a successful Hyde Park physician, came back from the central business district and spoke of passing Ed Debevic's, a popular middle-class restaurant: "I saw the yuppies and buppies standing in line just to get a hamburger. They were outside sipping wine and stuff waiting for their place. The guys stand around with their little coats over their shoulders. The modern black sees this and he thinks it's the thing to do. So there they are over at Ed Debevic's paying overprice for a hamburger."

This general image of the middle class is shared by many. Take Ted, for example, the fifty-five-year-old photographic technician who spent twenty years in the army before retiring to a civilian job. He makes fun of those who eat at Hyde Park's more upscale restaurants: "They go to Orly's restaurant for the bean sprouts, Mallory's for the brunch and stuff, and a menu they can't read, in French. It's cheap enough, but you can't read the menu. How do they order? You have to ask the waiter, 'Come here boy. What is that?' 'Well, sir, that's a hamburger!'" And Leroy, the electrician, says you wouldn't catch him next door at the Mellow Yellow; "The atmosphere is good there. But the blacks that come in, they figure that they are better than you. They want to be a little more sophisticated. And they're no better than me or you. I can go to the bakery and get me some crepes suzettes. I can ask for some crepes and make my own."

On one occasion, the man in the pink suit, who lived in a roach- and lice-infested room at a local hotel, observed a black couple that had just climbed out of a Mercedes convertible near the restaurant. As he sat by the window in Valois, he exclaimed: "If that boy was my son and he was making a hundred G's a year, I would sit him down and say, 'Son, save your money.' But after you're making that kind of dough, it's not the money anymore. It's a game for them. That's what they like. Because you can only have so much. How many cars can you buy?"

It seems to Slim and his sitting buddies that younger middle-class blacks have achieved their lot without having to struggle and without developing any character. J. J., a plasterer, once said: "I look at the middle-class black as being wealthy. But emotionally, physically, and mentally he cannot compete with me. I'm a more competitive individual than he is. I have never missed one day of work in forty years. When somebody asks me how long it will take to do a job, I tell them it will take just long enough to do it right the first time." There is marked revulsion at the disposition to take a better standard of living for granted, to strive to be sophisticated, and to spend money frivolously. As J. J. told me with a certain outrage on more than one occasion, "In terms of their wastefulness, there is very little difference between a middle-class black and a ghetto black."

Sometimes, amiable confrontations between members of the two groups occur in the cafeteria, with regulars usually getting the upper hand. Once, soon after the stock market crash of 1987, Ted asked Cornelius, the retired meter inspector known for his sarcastic wit, what he thought about the whole affair. Cornelius pointed to a black man wearing a suit and tie. "Don is a yuppie. So we can find out from him."

The man said he had no way to explain it. He asked Cornelius why he thought the market had crashed.

"What goes up must come down," Cornelius responded. Then, to tease the man in the suit, he asked, "How much did you lose?"

"I didn't lose anything," said the man.

"Oh, we know you lost something," responded an amused Cornelius.

But it is not only the wastefulness of the middle-class blacks that captures the attention of the men. Their outlook toward the black population of the area is also commonly expressed in statements about younger, lower-class blacks. Their resentment of these youths tends to revolve around differences in perspective that result from their age and particular experience. On one occasion, for example, a young black man known to work at a regular job but regarded as flashy was reproached for displaying an attitude the regulars regarded as dangerous: "Mike, what we don't like about your generation is that you are too open and aggressive. You walk around like a player and you take it all for granted. Forty years ago, open and aggressive could have cost me my life."[1] In such comments, the men appeal to their own experience as a way of setting themselves apart and feeling good about themselves. On another occasion, Al tried to explain to me why so few younger blacks come to the restaurant: "The younger ones don't come into Valois because they don't know how to communicate. They have never been exposed to shooting the shit in barbershops like the older generation."

Besides being criticized for their mode of dress, a general flashiness in their demeanor, and an inability to communicate, younger blacks are often accused of being unwilling to work. Once a few regulars were standing outside Valois listening to the White Sox game on Drake's little transistor radio. The radio was on the pavement, and the men were adjusting the long aerial for good reception when a group of black men in their early twenties passed by with a radio known variously as a boom box or a ghetto blaster. When the rap music playing on the big radio temporarily drowned out the transistor, the men were annoyed. Clarence, a sanitation worker, starting talking about some "young black cats" that worked on his shift on the airport run.

"They've had it on a silver platter. They walk into the place and they want to own it right now."

Claude, a cop, responded, "They are very unsatisfied. It's like 'You are making me do this.' Nobody is making you do anything. They want it on a silver platter and it's not there no longer."

Elvin, athletic looking at the age of sixty-eight, who had walked over to the group, interjected his opinion: "It all comes down to the computer and everything else. In our time we would do things with our hands. Manpower. Nobody has manpower anymore. The younger generations, if you make them lift fifty pounds, their backs hurt. We lifted hundreds of pounds and never thought nothing of it. It was like fun. And now if you tell kids to go get some groceries, they carry twenty-two pounds and they're tired."

Clarence said, looking at me, "It's funny. If you lived our generation and look at the new generation, it's so funny."

"No, it's sad," Elvin said. "Every young kid in school has either got a weapon, or dope, or he's gonna rob you. If he wants his fix he's gonna get you. It doesn't matter who you are. You can be his best friend, if he knows you've got money he'll kill you. It's nothing to him. Because he wants his fix."

The cop, Claude, observed, "In the older generations we didn't even drink a beer. If your mom and dad smelled a beer on you, oh my God, your mom would whip you, your daddy would whip you, and you might have to stay in for a year. Just go to school and come home and go to school and come back."

No doubt many of the characteristics of the younger generation disdained by the black regulars can be found in members of their own age group as well. But the regulars rarely refer to their own generation, except as a homogeneous group above reproach. Their resentment is directed chiefly at middle-class blacks and younger poor blacks, the groups guilty, as they see it, of flashiness, wastefulness, and laziness. In such conversations the participants shift back and forth between assuming that the problems of black people are due to shortcomings of individuals and are rooted in the organization of the larger society.[2] Many such comments, if made by a group of white men, would be labeled racist by middle-class observers.[3] But the men at Valois are not in the habit of pulling punches, even when it comes to their own people. They exhibit many of the attitudes one would expect from a group of working-class white men, especially in their views about American society and government, child rearing and discipline, about the welfare system, democracy, and authority. Although these men are strongly antagonistic toward the political right, they hold the same belief in personal responsibility that many white conservative Democrats and Republicans do.

Here are some typical views of the problems associated with social programs, illegitimacy, and dependency. Ted, Cornelius, and Walter, a musician, were talking about conditions in the ghetto.

"I don't understand what happened here in Chicago," Cornelius said. "We used to be a solid group of people."

Ted responded that it all started "with the good President Johnson. I was in the army and I hear, 'You are socioeconomically underprivileged.' Not me. I ate three meals every day."

Cornelius said, "Then there was the giveaway programs when we started being given things free. We never needed that."

Ted agreed. "Girls did not get pregnant back then. If they did they were shipped down South to some relatives somewhere. The baby was left there. They came back and they went to school. And then after they got out of school it was okay to have babies."

A few days later I challenged Ted on some of the things that I had heard. It was clear that he felt justified in his views: "We don't approve for good reasons. A girl doesn't like her mother telling her to come in at 11:00. She gets pregnant and she can get on welfare, get her own apartment. This is not good. Then you have another baby. . . . There was harder times. There was less social programs in my day and everybody made it. Everybody made it."

Months later, Slim and Ted were talking about many of these same issues while I was at the table. Whereas on the earlier occasion I had been merely sitting close by as an observer, this time the remarks were directed at me. Slim said, "They did have a thing the same as welfare. It was called relief. Now that was a shame. To be on relief. People walked around looking down on you. Nowadays some of them think, 'Well, the money's out there. We may as well get it.'"

Ted added, "We are of a completely different world. We always were. We had a paper route and we would deliver papers twice a day. You got up at four o'clock in the morning, ran down to the branch, picked them up, made the run in the morning before you went to school. Then after school you went and got your second batch for the day and threw those. You'd go through the alley throwing them on both sides. Or you worked the grocery stores delivering groceries. Helping the guys clean up the stores or unload the trucks. You always had a job. Sit around waiting on a check? Oh, man!" The past is a pervasive reference point for many of the opinions to which the black regulars cling. Phrases such as "We used to be a solid group of people" and "Back in our day . . ." are constantly repeated to make the contrast between then and now. In addition to beliefs about welfare and dependency, images of the past are used to legitimate views on discipline, child rearing, and authority. These field notes synthesize a variety of concerns:

> Ozzie, a social worker, was talking about discipline to Harold and Cornelius when Slim made this comment to a chorus of nodding heads: "The greatest mistake we ever made was wanting our kids to have more than we had. That is wrong. Kid gotta work. Kid gotta understand what money is and what money does and how you get through the world without it. But as soon as it's given, it's expected: You can't say 'Here's your allowance until you're one hundred years old.' Kids stay with parents now until they are thirty."
>
> Cornelius agreed: "That's the problem with the aid. People expect it."

On another occasion, Leroy, an electrician, and Willis, a carpenter, were talking about their common experiences as children in Chicago. Leroy said, "When I was coming up I played out in the vacant lot. I shot marbles. I played with yo-yos."

Willis concurred, "Yeah, I used to shoot marbles too, Leroy. Now these youngsters are shooting pistols and shooting dope. I can't understand it."

"I can't understand it either," Leroy said. "It's a different environment."

Months later, the black regulars discussed a song by the Temptations about the singer Marvin Gaye, who had been murdered by his father. Many of them felt little sympathy for him. Whereas others mourned the singer, these men focused on the fact that Gaye was reputed to have provoked his father by hitting him.

"In black families it used to be that you wouldn't hit your father. That's your *father*," Slim said.

Ted suggested that this was similar to a case in Chicago where a woman was accused of having hit her grandson. "This little social worker had a grandmother in front of the judge, who was black. And she said, 'She beat him unmercifully.' She wanted the court to take the kid from the grandmother. And the judge said to the grandmother, 'What did the child do?' Grandmama said, 'I came out from the bathroom and I caught him with his hands in my purse.' 'Say what?' said the judge. 'Case dismissed.' The little social worker was enraged. 'This is brutality.' Judge said, 'You do not understand the black experience. You do not steal from your grandmother. That is the one looking after you. And he steals from his grandmother? I ought to put him in jail. Case dismissed.'"

Slim responded, "In our generation parents did what they called hands-on raising. Your mother and father put their hand on you."

Ted added, "I remember my grandmother came up from Mississippi to watch us when our parents went away. And I remember I said to her, 'You can't tell me what to do.' She was just shocked that I had the nerve to tell her that. She said, 'Son, I'm your grandmother. I used to hit your mother. You know what I'll do to you? I'll kill you.'"

Slim agreed that too many homes are run like a democracy. "People think that the whole world should be run like a democracy. Police shouldn't be allowed to be rough with criminals. Parents shouldn't be allowed to hit children."

Ted said, "What keeps a democracy free are not democratic things. Families that raise good citizens are not democratic. The police and the army are not democratic either."

A strong belief in deference to authority does not imply an automatic trust of institutions. To the contrary, the black regulars tend to be very cynical about the motives of the powerful institutions of their society. It is not surprising, therefore, that one of the beliefs they hold is that the world they live in is controlled and manipulated by powers at the top. Such forces are usually institutions as vague as "government" or as specific as the CIA. When a man suggests that nothing is an accident, he is making reference to the "fact" that important events are brought about by those who hold the reins of power. It is commonly asserted, for example, that Martin Luther King was assassinated in a government conspiracy. It is taken for granted that society is run by a set of elites and institutions that arrange the most important events. A general cynicism dictates that these institutions are fundamentally dishonest. This note, recorded after a World Series game, is illustrative:

> A man will sometimes claim that because the bottom line of professional sports is money, the series usually goes as many as six games, often seven. The series is fixed, and the players do what they are told in order to bring in the most revenue for major league baseball. This was the view when the Mets won the sixth game, scoring three runs in the bottom half of the ninth inning with two men out and nobody on base. The Red Sox had committed so many fielding errors that it seemed obvious to the black regulars that the series had been fixed.
>
> When the series was over, Cornelius said in a loud voice, "That series was rigged. Bill Buckner [the Boston first baseman, who made a crucial error] got some big money in a Swiss bank account." Nodding heads and laughter greeted his comment.

It is a short step from such beliefs to the statements by many in the black community that drugs and AIDS were planted in the ghettos as part of government attempts at genocide, though many of these men would not endorse that view. Indeed, public opinion polls among blacks indicate that there is great uncertainty about whether white society is engaged in a conspiratorial plot to eliminate ghetto dwellers.[4] Charges of racial genocide take various forms. AIDS is viewed as a form of racial warfare, a virus created in a government or CIA laboratory in an attempt to "clean up" a seemingly dirty population. Drug availability in ghettos is seen as a deliberate plot to wreak havoc on black communities by progressively weakening the population of those districts: the earlier policy of "dumping" liquor on the Indian reservations is likened to the government's weak efforts to stop the flow of drugs to the inner city. The war with Iraq was seen as an effort to eliminate the race by placing a disproportionate number of young black men on the front lines. Efforts to improve birth control are viewed as attempts to sterilize the black population. Attempts to encourage transracial adoptions constitute cultural genocide. The infant mortality rate among blacks—twice that of whites—is taken as evidence for the wider society's deliberate policy. The disproportionate number of billboards advertising cigarettes and liquor in ghetto districts shows that blacks are targeted for early death.

Yet, the belief that society is run by forces at the top is not synonymous with uncertainty about acts of mass genocide. Many of the black regulars at Valois will smile and laugh at the "silliness" of such notions, quickly reminding the genocide theorist that black people are choosing to take the drugs themselves. Some believe "it's a product of a degenerate society." Others will say that they don't know for sure if the government is responsible, but that any nation that can send men to the moon could stop drugs from reaching the ghettos if it wanted to. Still, another group will boldly support any view that accords with the general distrust of government and institutions. In this respect, these cafeteria men are typical of the larger black population, which feels a great deal of uncertainty about these issues.

More typical of the plots perceived by the black regulars is the hypothesis arrived at by Slim and Harold in a discussion about a murder that had occurred a few blocks away. I was sitting at the next table when Harold declared that the story would never make the papers. Slim seemed to agree and the conversation was about to change to another topic when I asked Harold why he would say such a thing.

Slim answered, "Well, of course it isn't in the papers, Mitch. They're not allowed to write about that."

I asked, "But who can stop them?"

"The university," Willie chimed in from afar. "The University of Chicago is one of the biggest powers in the city. They have money in all the right places. They don't want no stories about Hyde Park ruining the reputation of the area."

Like residents of black neighborhoods in many American cities, the ghetto dwellers on the South Side of Chicago live under the dominating presence of a large university that arouses various feelings of deference, suspicion, and resentment in a black population.[5] In Hyde Park, interaction between poor blacks and members of the university community is common. The normal distrust of institutions is expressed with particular vehemence. Frequently, for example, black men suggest with great resentment that the university instills fear of neighborhood blacks in its students. Proud of living in accordance with the pattern of moral values embodied in their own notions of respectability, they believe that the fear felt by students causes them to be treated as persons of lesser moral worth. Ozzie once put it this way: "The university gets those students in rap sessions. They tell them not to travel alone. They get these white students when they come here from Boston and New York or wherever and they get 'em in those lectures [raising his voice, imitating an imaginary professor], 'When you go out into the neighborhood, you travel in groups. Be careful who you talk to.'" Others, such as Luther, the newsstand attendant, sometimes speak with outrage about the buses the

university uses to transport its students through the neighborhood, both day and night:

> The buses are offensive. I hate them because we know
> what they are. Ride around in a bus with the light out.
> What is that saying to black folks? A group of white kids is
> walking together and they see me, all of them, they
> huddle together. Well, I'm afraid of them as they are of
> me. Years ago they used to talk to you. Blacks and whites
> used to have friendships. They used to party together.
> Now white women are scared. They see a black dude and
> they turn away or run. Because the university throws that
> into their minds. You want to put fear into everybody? I
> have heard some radical blacks in this neighborhood say
> they would like to throw a bomb in those buses. And be-
> lieve me, as the races become more polarized, one day
> they will. What are these buses saying? That people in
> the neighborhood are murderers, rapists, and thieves.
> When you travel in big buses and turn the lights off inside
> what are you telling me? Who are those lights turned off
> for, you or me? Those white students should think about
> it when they get on that bus.

Other hostile remarks are directed at the lack of integration
at the university and in the campus police, which, after the
Vatican's, is widely reputed among the black regulars to be the
largest private patrol force in the world. Many men, like Ozzie,
charge that campus police monitor black movement in the
Hyde Park neighborhood. He speaks with resentment of the
fact that most of the officers he sees are black:

> On the staff of the university they have mostly black
> police but not but a few black professors. What does that
> tell you? That's not telling you that you are integrated in
> that school. Hell, you're not integrated! They have black
> people for their own protection. Let me tell you about
> campus security. I notice they pick up white women and
> take them to their houses. This is what I've noticed

through the years. The campus police wait outside these coffee shops, these bookstores, and they follow the students home for protection. And if you are black, and they don't know you, they follow you. And they get your license number. They do a lot of double-dealing over there and the people know it. The University of Chicago has a bad image among the intelligent and not so intelligent black people. They resent them. But they resent them for the things that they are fostering. They have fostered this. Nobody likes the U. of C. police because they harass black people. Black policemen harass black people. It's no different than South Africa. Sometimes the black police officers come up to you and they'll say, "How's things going in the neighborhood?" They want to get information out of you. I just say, "I wouldn't know. I stay here all the time." I'd love to have a conversation with Levi [former president of the university who some black regulars believe is still president] and all those guys over there that run the university.

Finally, some hostility is directed at the student newspaper, the *Maroon*, which is distributed throughout the neighborhood and which publishes crime maps indicating with stars and dots neighborhood blocks where various crimes have been committed. Ozzie says that some of the regulars find these maps offensive:

Those people sit in those ivory towers like Levi and Kleinbard [a university vice-president]. They think we don't know. I read you, Kleinbard. I read you in the papers. The University of Chicago papers. I look at that crime map they throw up there. [He is chuckling.] You think people aren't observing. You think that people don't know what is going on. The map says, "Two rapes happened here last month." [Laughing] It is an insult. So then you get these white girls walking on the street and when they see a black they run. The university tells them you'll be raped. They pass you and they look at you like you're gonna harm them.

Sometimes, especially when a black regular feels uncomfortable or challenged by members of the university community, there are incidents of subtle conflict in the cafeteria. Sexton, a student, sat down at a table where Willie and Cecil, a bill collector, were talking. The restaurant had been crowded and he stood with his tray for quite a while before he sat down. It was obvious to Willie and Cecil that the youngster was sitting with them only out of necessity. He was friendly when he joined them, immediately asking a number of questions to show his interest. He began by asking Cecil what he did for a living. Then he asked Willie. Things seemed to be going pretty smoothly until he asked the men whether they had any children.

Willie and Cecil both said no. The young man looked perplexed, perhaps because both men were in their sixties.

"Really?" he asked, surprised.

The men were offended. In a loud voice, Ted interjected from another table with a response I had heard before, "No and none of that 'not that you know of' stuff. We don't know of any because there are none."

At this point Willie, who was somewhat irritated, decided to try to show the student up.

"Say, young man, I see you know something about music," he said, pointing to some sheet music that the boy had with him. As other regulars watched from their tables, Willie told the boy that back in the good old days he had been arranging music for Duke Ellington and playing with Count Basie. "You know the chord on that song?" he asked the student. "That's me."

After the student had asked questions excitedly for about fifteen minutes, he went away. Apparently he hadn't realized that the regulars had been "playing" with him. The men at the other tables all had smirks on their faces.

Clarence yelled out, "Now I say this boy is in college. He

supposed to have some brains in his head." Then he imitated the young man. "You did what? You played with whom?"[6]

On another occasion, two "lifetime students," Jim and Sam, were sitting at a table trying to figure out how to move a piece of used furniture that one of them had recently purchased. Jim said, "No matter how you cut it, it's still gonna be a certain length."

Sam responded, "Wait, tell me how to figure it out."

Jim said, "You see, the problem is, the real issue is, how tight the corners are. But I don't know exactly how to figure the dimensions."

He began drawing a diagram of the building on a paper napkin.

"Okay. We've got the stairway here," Jim said as he waved the napkin in the air. Now, we've got a stairway going up, then a flat landing, then another staircase. Now this is eighty-six inches."

"What's the width?" asked Sam.

"Oh, the width is like twenty-eight. But how do I figure out what the height has to be for it to clear?"

"I don't know how to do that mathematically," answered Sam.

"I'll have to ask Dorsen, my mathematician friend, to figure it out for me," said Jim.

After they left the cafeteria, Ted commented on what he had heard: "It's all right to be all whippy do up there, but they make a career of it. There are so many of these guys around that it's pathetic. You got all these people with all their great knowledge and they can't do anything. They can't figure out how to move a simple piece of furniture. What do we do with these guys? I don't care how much they know, there's no place for them, because there's too many philosophers and there's too many physicists. Even if they graduate, none of them have jobs."

Willie disagreed. "That is not true," he said. "These people will go to Washington, D.C., and formulate national policy. What do they call them? The yuppies? There's a lot of that. It's here. I see them all over the place. Their families are rich. They own big estates. What do they care about our life? They want to be bank corporate presidents and formulate policy and things like that."

Incidents like these are relatively rare. But at times, when they feel they are witnessing stupidity or being put on the spot or treated in a manner inappropriate to their moral worth, it is not unusual for them to respond by denigrating another person's knowledge, as Clarence did when he imitated the college boy's naïveté. Common sense, they believe, is more profound than what one learns from books.

Rather than withdrawing altogether from social contacts with people who have different beliefs and values, the men seem to feel a need to be near them, even if that means sometimes differentiating and defending themselves. In the process, they often fall back on common memories and their own high regard for experience. "Go live it, son," or "Experience gives you a point to make," or "If all a person knows is what he reads" are phrases repeated over and over in conversations that focus legitimacy on beliefs and values drawn from memories. The black regulars have nostalgic images of respectability that make them conceive of themselves as unusual. As Officer Wilkins says, "People who been around and seen everything, we want a place to meet. We don't want to be with people who are gonna tell us what they think they know. We can tell each other what we do know."

The regulars also tend to be notably cynical in discussions about politics. They respect Franklin Delano Roosevelt, whose social programs and recognition of blacks won over many northern blacks to the Democratic party in the 1930s.[7] They disdain Ronald Reagan, who still symbolizes racism, "savage cuts," greed, and "the rich getting richer." One day, at the height of the Iran-Contra controversy, a middle-class black man sat down with Cornelius, the retired meter inspector, and me. He mentioned that President Reagan would be holding a press conference that evening. Cornelius's response is illustrative of the cynical attitude: "Reagan is a liar. He creates disharmony. Those reporters can't get no answers from him. He don't know nothing. Reagan don't know nothing. This country don't have nothing but a bag of credit cards. And would Reagan wage a war in the Persian Gulf with a bag of credit cards? He says he didn't know we sold weapons to Iran. That's the biggest lie I ever knew. Unless he's the dumbest president we've ever had."

The middle-class black man began to disagree: "Now wait a minute . . ."

Cornelius interrupted: "Are you a conservative?"

"Am I . . . ?"

"I just want to know if you in the middle of the road, or if you right or left. If you can't bend or if you can roll with the punches. I just want to know, are you a conservative or a liberal?"

The man hesitated.

"Well, Cornelius . . ."

"You a little of both?"

"Yeah."

"Well, then, you not die-hard conservative."

In addition to the cynicism which marks a difference between the two groups, this conversation also typifies the wariness and intolerance with which some seeming right-wingers are approached in conversation. Like most of his friends at the cafeteria, Cornelius is willing to discuss amiably a range of issues, but the legitimacy of the political right is not among them. It is important to him to be part of a consensual collectivity. Yet once a man's political credentials are established, he can express any view with impunity and on any particular issue there is always a wide spectrum of opinion. Thus, Smith, a carpenter, expressed this view to me in front of his respectful sitting buddies: "I'm against reverse discrimination. You had nothing to do with the blacks coming out of Africa. If he wants to blame someone let him blame the black who sold him into slavery." Indeed, affirmative action is highly controversial, especially when a man believes it holds him back or creates an unjust system. Once Harold said to Black, "Hey, you know that first black woman who they put on the back of a garbage truck? Know where she's at now?"

"Uh, Harold, is she a boss?"

"She's got her own office and department," Harold responded.

"It's supposed to go by seniority," Black said. "But they will go and get a woman and move her up!"

Indeed, the black regulars share many conservative social opinions with those ethnic whites who believe that the stability of their local community is threatened by a poverty culture and affirmative action.[8] Yet unlike the so-called Reagan Democrats, those whites whose political allegiances shifted dramatically away from liberalism during the 1980s, these poor and working-class black men remain antagonistic to symbols of Republican conservatism. Though they are forthright about the failures and abuses of the war on poverty, and cynical about the motives of those who would do good, they still have mostly leftward leaning views on foreign policy and an overriding belief in the legitimacy of collectivistic liberalism.

The weight of their opinions suggests that Slim and his buddies believe that what makes them stand out from others in the black belt who share their views on many issues is their readiness to affirm the value of personal responsibility with overwhelming self-confidence. The men at Slim's table are sensitive to their own separateness when behaving in accordance with specific ideas of moral worth. They live with an acute sense of moral isolation.

Membership in Society

CHAPTER

5

Openness

One particular set of incidents illustrates that, unlike typical images of urban dwellers, the black regulars at Valois were not merely guardians of turf, attempting to maintain and reinforce expectations about themselves and others.[1] They were creatures of sociability for whom contact with the wider circle of cafeteria groups was a source of gratification. This was particularly evident during a short period when the restaurant closed down.

While the business had always been profitable, the Greek owners knew how "See Your Food" was perceived by the majority of community residents who weren't "in the know." The restaurant was in poor repair. Its run-down appearance served to create and reinforce its image as a hangout for down-and-outers. Spiro and Gus knew that while some people treasured Valois because it was old and simple, others kept their distance because it was dirty and dilapidated. As time wore on, the status of the cafeteria as the oldest restaurant in Hyde Park had become for the Greeks more a source of embarrassment than a source of pride.

For most of a week in the middle of February, they closed for remodeling. During this period, the wider social world of Valois, constituted of black regulars, old-time white regulars, and lifetime students, began to exhibit an intense and explicit recognition of itself as a collectivity. In Wendy's, the local Harper Square restaurant, and on the street, small cliques of habitués, black and white, waved and nodded to one another, through windows and around booths. This collective consciousness replaced the indifference that had previously characterized relations between many of the smaller cliques in the restaurant. Members of these cliques now demonstrated a civil attachment to one another, founded upon the recognition of common participation in the Valois way of life.

The ongoing social world of Valois was normally constituted of certain expectations of a particular physical arrangement of persons and groups—not only of the black regulars but of the larger population that frequented the cafeteria. These men knew one another by sight and sometimes greeted one another, although physical spacing tended to keep them separate from day to day. Each group sat in its own part of the cafeteria, and habitués knew this arrangement. Under normal circumstances it was very unusual for a regular to upset expectations and sit somewhere new.

Whereas inside the cafeteria many people of different groups did not know one another, the exodus from Valois provided a basis for conversation that had not existed before. The following incident is representative of many that occurred during that week.

Harry, an older white man who usually rode with the meat-packer, Werner Mandlebaum, came into Wendy's, where some of the black regulars were sitting. I later confirmed that Harry hadn't been in the habit of speaking to any black man at Valois. Now, when he sat down at the next table, the regulars turned and said hello.

Looking at a man he usually only nodded to now and then, Harry said, "You got your hair cut. Just in time to be eating at Wendy's."

The other black men laughed, and the man Harry had addressed said, "Boss got tired of me having the longest hair in the place. It was between me and a white guy, but the white guy got his hair cut and I decided I better get mine cut."

For that moment, they seemed like old friends. The conversation drifted into a discussion about video recorders in which the black regulars shared with Harry some information they had on the latest models. By the time the white man was eating the apple dumpling that he had for dessert, he moved over to the same table as the black man he had first spoken to. When he got up to leave, the regulars said, "See you tomorrow" and he returned their good-bye.

Even more common were situations in which men would enter Wendy's and, in the process of searching for friends, say hello to patrons from the cafeteria they had never greeted before. Or people who hadn't addressed each other in the past would stand outside Valois together, engaging in running commentary on the construction that was taking place inside. Whereas normally proximity was taken for granted without salutations or conversation, now co-presence was a foundation for new personal associations.

The single most important prop for maintaining the usual order of relations at Valois was the pattern of spatial relations whereby black regulars settled near the windows and smaller white cliques sat back by the counter. Through the period of adjusting to the physical order at Wendy's and Harper Square, such socially erected barriers between different cliques were breached. For the first time there was substantial contact between some of the white cliques and the larger collectivity of black men, with whom they did not normally associate. It was evident that many patrons derived a particular satisfaction from the reduction of social distance. Rather than attempting to remain among their own groups, in their "places," they seized the opportunity to get to know members of the larger collectivity a little better. They obviously felt gratified to have contact with other habitués in the larger group and the feeling was mutual.

This episode indicates that openness, sociability, and the desire to be part of the larger society are important dimensions of the conduct of cafeteria life. Respectability did not assume its highest form in stereotypes and contrasts with those who could somehow be deemed inferior to those making the comparisons. The public cafeteria was a locale where barriers that normally divided and isolated people could sometimes break down. Even when physical spacing erected barriers between groups, there were still situations in which patrons often interacted outside of their normal social positions.

The relationship between Chicago police officers and other patrons in the cafeteria offers an example. Valois was one of a few restaurants on the South Side that had evolved into a hangout for many Twenty-first District patrolmen during their mealtime breaks. When police officers pass a restaurant that has many squad cars parked outside, they can be confident that the food inside will be both hearty and inexpensive. They also know, of course, that the clientele will include fellow police officers—a consideration important to some of them.

"You like to be among policemen or among people who understand policemen," Officer Murphy said. "You like to be able to talk freely without somebody going back and saying, 'I don't like what he says. He's a policeman.' If a bunch of policemen go in there, we understand what's going on. And other kinds of people, they understand over a period of time what's going on. They know how to blend in. They get to the point where they understand our hurts, our wants, and our needs and that life goes on even though we have a policeman in here."

As Officer Murphy's words suggest, the occupational world of the police is one of much solidarity and clear distinctions between us and them. Many officers believe that only other cops can understand the difficult conditions under which they work, and some trust very few civilians. They know that the public, especially in black communities, often feel uncomfortable in their presence.[2] At Valois, by contrast, many of the police were actually regarded as fellow cafeteria men by the group of black regulars. The police experienced a sort of companionship there that they rarely found in other places.

Some black cafeteria men were among the few civilians with whom typical police distinctions between us and them effectively broke down. Cops who had been driving with the same partner for many hours sometimes preferred to take a break from their colleague so that they could sit alone or "shoot the shit" with some of the other customers. Over a period of time, a police officer would come to know a large number of regular customers. Such interaction provided an important kind of companionship to a man whose uniform usually erected a barrier between himself and those members of the community whom he controlled and regulated.

Sometimes an officer would encounter in the cafeteria a man with whom he had had a run-in on some previous occasion, a man who resented the officer for having enforced a minor ordinance. On other occasions, the police would unexpectedly come upon men at Valois whom they had had to lock up for more serious offenses. Officer Johnson was sitting at a table for two. I was sitting at the next table. We had been chatting back and forth when Green, a man who was known to have been imprisoned in the past for armed robbery, walked through the door. He had been out of jail for over a year, working a regular job cleaning out the currency exchanges on Forty-seventh Street. When he spotted Johnson, he looked a bit startled. When he took his food from the counter he walked over to the table where Johnson was seated.

"Mind if I have a seat?" he asked the officer.

"It's a public restaurant."

As the two men talked, their relationship became clear.

When their discussion was winding down, Johnson said, "Let's face it. I had to do what I had to do. What would you have done in that situation?"

"I would have killed you."

"But are you dead?"

Green laughed nervously and said, "No, you right. You right, Johnson. I know I was wrong."

After Green left, I asked Officer Johnson about the conversation. He said, "I just wanted to explain to the man. I made him understand why I had to do what I had to do. I have a job to do and, the things he did, I had no choice. Maybe he's a good man in bad circumstances. But we is both human. I always try to make people understand why I have to do what I have to do."

It was significant that this encounter took place in a public cafeteria. When Green asked Officer Johnson if he could sit down, the patrolman's answer, "It's a public restaurant," unenthusiastic as it was, made it plain that the man's presence at his table would not be viewed as an encroachment. Valois provided occasions for interaction between people who would not normally have an opportunity to talk, much less take a meal together. Unlike many restaurants in which an individual's table or booth is symbolic of a certain territorial exclusiveness, the unrestricted, open nature of public space in the cafeteria gave license to a man who had been convicted of a crime to be seated with the very police officer who had arrested him. He could transcend his stigma, putting it behind him if only for those moments, and the cop could transcend his role. In telling me some of the things he had said to Green, the officer emphasized that they were both "only human." In the cafeteria, companionship sometimes consisted of the affirmation of the reality of a self that existed, not as a function of role or status, but as a mere consequence of one's humanity.

It would trivialize relations at Valois to suggest that their sole function in the lives of regulars was to heighten a "consciousness of kind." To be sure, discussions about memories and beliefs often served no other purpose than to remind regulars that they were different from other types of people. But participation in cafeteria life also enabled a man to achieve a greater sense of his own worth through positive contact with members of other groups.

CHAPTER

6

The Need for Contact with Society

On one of my first evenings at "See Your Food," a hefty black man stumbled in, demanding money from customers. It was 9:00 o'clock, and I was the only white left among the patrons. The drunkard's loud, boisterous manner startled me, but I was relieved by the sight of police officers just a few tables away. Slim, Harold, and Earl, sitting in a corner, ignored the man by simply staring right through him.

The drunkard approached Spiro, one of the Greek owners, who stood behind the steam table. I kept my eyes on the police, assuming they would rush to his assistance. But when Spiro told the man to get out and he refused, it was the Greek who came from behind the counter to escort him to the door. Only half the size of the physically intimidating drunk, Spiro approached him with the confidence of a fighter who had waged many such battles.

I glanced at the police in disbelief. Why didn't they stand up to protect the owner?

Spiro yanked the man. He resisted, but Spiro prevailed.

When the man was finally out the door, he fell and lay on the sidewalk in front of the restaurant. Like the officers, the men at Slim's table casually observed the incident and then returned to their conversation. On leaving the cafeteria, each of them would step over the man's body.

After all the customers had gone, Spiro cleaned the steam

table. I asked him why the police officers hadn't offered any assistance. He said that all he had to do was ask. "I know this guy and they know him too. We have trouble with him a lot. Tomorrow he'll come in and act perfectly normal. He won't even remember what happened. When I remind him, he'll draw a blank."

A few days later another troublemaker was put out for making a scene. He had walked up to the table of a man sitting with his girlfriend and tried to flirt with the woman. Having little success, he turned around to the water dispenser and filled a glass for himself. The man at the table was clearly enraged. Picking up a chair, he sneaked up behind the troublemaker and struck him on the head. This time all the customers, black and white, seemed startled. When Spiro and Gus, the two owners, saw what had happened, they knew whose fault it had been. The man on the floor had a long record of disturbing customers. They ordered him to leave and not return.

During the late seventies and early eighties, scenes of this kind occurred often at Valois, as they did in many establishments in the nearby ghetto.[1] But later the troublemakers learned that this run-down cafeteria was no longer their domain. After working in the kitchen for many years, Spiro and Gus saved their money and purchased the restaurant in the late seventies, determined not to let their investment disintegrate into a circus environment. With their crew of tough-minded, stubborn Greeks they devoted themselves to maintaining a state of absolute order at Valois. These immigrant Greeks have created an environment conducive to the collective life of the black men. Under the Greeks' dominion, the cafeteria remains attractive to a diverse clientele, including middle-class white residents of the Hyde Park community. For the black regulars, it embodies the order and diversity of a wider society.

Most of those who work to maintain such an environment at Valois are from a small village in southern Greece near Tripoli, called Akladhokampos.[2] Spiro and Gus, men in their forties, grew up in the village and attended elementary school together. Like many immigrants, they came to America in pursuit of a higher living standard. The Greeks know that in their pursuit of material advancement they have sacrificed a peaceful existence in their village for the task of maintaining order on the outskirts of the ghetto. Besides their work behind the counter or in the kitchen, they routinely have to quell disturbances that are often upsetting and sometimes dangerous. There is a time when every Greek laboring in the cafeteria wants to give it all up for the sweet and simple pleasures of the village he left behind.

Tim, twenty-nine, is strong and bulky, of a saturnine disposition. After the owners, he has the most seniority among the Greeks and is in charge when neither Spiro nor Gus can be there. Like Spiro, Tim is known for his audacity with the hoodlums, and many avoid the place when they see him behind the counter. On one occasion, two young black men walked into Valois, apparently intoxicated. Tim ordered them out before they neared the steam table. They were irate, yet defensive, claiming they had not been drinking. Tim raised his voice and reiterated his command. One flung his change furiously at the steam table. As coins flew under the glass and landed in the roast beef, they walked out. Later, I mentioned to Tim that he had seemed bold and uncompromising earlier in the evening. He said, "In the beginning when I came to America I was asking myself, 'Can I talk to a guy like this?' I would say, 'No, I can't talk like that.' But now I can. I definitely can. Oh, yeah. As I tell you, the first thing you learn is how to be playing it tough."

Tim's younger brother, Yiannis, works the cash register in the mornings. After graduating from high school in Chicago he started at Valois. The time he spends behind the counter, dealing with the public, has given him a mature demeanor disproportionate to his age—eighteen. He often handles the public with the same toughness as his older brother. One day, for example, a man came into the cafeteria and accused the Greeks of owing him five dollars.

"When I left this morning, you forgot to give me five dollars change back."

"What's the problem?" Yiannis muttered, as a long line of patrons waited for him to ring their orders.

"When I went back home I called you and asked about the five dollars. But you couldn't remember anything about the whole thing so you told me to talk to you. I want my five bucks back."

Yiannis remembered the telephone call, but he had long ago learned not to be pushed around. He decided that the man was being too forceful, presumptuous, and rude, even if his story was true.

"Listen," he said, "I gonna do something simple. When I go upstairs tonight to count the money, if it's over, I promise you since you come here every day I gonna give it to you."

The customer responded angrily, "It doesn't matter if you find it or not; it's five bucks and it's mine."

Having overheard the conversation, Spiro approached the customer courteously and said, "I'm sorry that you have a problem, but it's not my cashier's fault. When you leave the register, you're supposed to count your change."

Yiannis continued ringing up the long line of trays.

Having turned a deaf ear, the man repeated his demand: "It doesn't matter if the money is short or over. I want my five bucks back because it's mine. If you don't give it to me, I'm not going to come back here again."

Spiro looked at the man as if to ask, "Is that a threat or a promise?"

When the man walked out, Yiannis explained, "It's not the five dollars. It's his attitude."

Spiro agreed.

Vassili, Spiro's nephew, came to Chicago to take a bachelor's degree in computer science from the University of Illinois. He is living in America on a student visa. He fills in sporadically on weekends, whenever his uncle needs someone to take over the cash register. When Vassili first started working at the cafeteria, he was taken aback to see "bums with shirts off and holes in their pants" coming into a public restaurant. He was startled, too, to see the disrespectful way in which such people were treated by the Greeks who then owned the establishment. "When I came from Greece, on my first day at Valois, they had to kick a customer out. They were very hard on him and I couldn't understand how a person, even a bum, could take that. If someone talked to me in such a way, I would never take it. It didn't seem human. But after you are here a while, you begin to realize that . . . sometimes they don't react like you do. So it makes you tough."

Like many of the men who work at the cafeteria, it is difficult for Vassili to separate himself in his own mind from the role that he occupies in maintaining order: "The reason it hurts comes with direct communication with people. It's not like you stay behind the counter and you're not familiar with the whole thing. You're part of the whole thing. You are not working like a manager in a big restaurant. The manager, what he does when the people come in, he puts them in their seats and gives them the menu and walks away. And in the end he's gonna say good-bye and that's it. But in the cafeteria you not only serve the food, you take the money, and you'll be seeing these people two or three times every day. You see these people when they come up to the counter and you start talking to them. You come to feel with these people."

Although it is sometimes personally difficult for these Greeks to maintain their tough stance, they do so in the belief that an orderly environment is essential to the conduct of a healthy business. At the same time, the black regulars have contact with the larger society through their participation in the standards the Greeks maintain. That public order is a valued dimension of the wider world for Slim and his sitting buddies. As Officer Wilkens tells me, "At other restaurants that I'll be going to, the people act like a bunch of motherfuckers. In fact, you can see some of the same people who come here at other places and they'll be acting completely different. The same people. It's sort of like a transition. You got one place you go, you act accordingly. Another restaurant you go, it doesn't make any difference. You want to tap dance on the table, you get up and dance. There are a lot of places where you can let the Indian out of you. But not here."

What is it about the cafeteria that makes it a haven for men who seek an orderly environment? Part of the answer lies in the existence of a set of expectations that guide behavior there. Because Valois is located a few blocks outside the ghetto, the principles that control conduct in the cafeteria are regarded by many black men as their own, but now more than ever embodied in the white world. As Murphy told me, "This restaurant is a place where a woman with a baby can come and not be accosted by some black cat. Even though they are here, they know that there are certain things they cannot do at Valois in front of white folks that they can do elsewhere. They know to hide their whiskey bottles, even when they are standing outside Valois. They know that they can't play the boom box as loud on the street outside Valois as on Forty-seventh Street. There's more surveillance, and they know what's accepted."

Even some of the unemployed street corner men who come to the cafeteria—people who act differently at other places—assume the attitudes of the "white world" as principles to guide their conduct in the cafeteria. The "white world" functions as a vague generality, not unlike someone looking over your shoulder or a "public" in whose presence it is firmly understood that one should not wash his dirty laundry.[3] For many men, it is intrinsically satisfying to enter into a positive relationship with society by participating in an orderly environment of that wider world.

In this context the black regulars are also sometimes in the presence of celebrities and politicians, the kinds of people in whom it is imagined that the power of society resides. Some men place great importance on this aspect of the cafeteria, as when Cecil describes his relationships with the gangster Flukey Stokes and the former owner of the Chicago White Sox, Bill Veeck: "I knew Flukey. He had a big bracelet. That bracelet used to be worth about ten thousand dollars. He had rings on his fingers worth five thousand dollars. He had a Cadillac limo that he used to ride here in. I'd say, 'Hey, Fluke, how you doing?' He'd say, 'I'm doing fine.' Bill Veeck: I've talked to him. I once asked him why he gave up the Sox. He said, 'I just got tired.' He knew me by name because I told him my name. He was very friendly."

Contact with Flukey Stokes and with such important blacks as Muhammad Ali and the late Mayor Harold Washington, who had also patronized the restaurant over the years, provides the regulars with a means of entering into a more affirmative relationship with the mainstream, emblematic as these individuals are of their society. It is the order and power embodied in that wider world, rather than the usual skin color of its mainstream institutions, that attracts some men from the ghetto to the cafeteria.

In addition to the black celebrities that regulars sometimes encounter, there are lesser-known whites who are thought to represent dimensions of the power structure of the local community: the wealthy businessman George Gladis, owner of the gigantic One-Stop supermarket in a slum nearby and a partner in the restaurant of Mike Ditka, coach of the Chicago Bears; the meat-packer Werner Mandlebaum, founder and proprietor of Chicago's last slaughterhouse; Morton Fruchtman, a successful Hyde Park landlord with a reputation among the regulars as one of the few local realtors who won't rent an apartment he wouldn't live in himself; Timothy Goodsell, president of the Hyde Park Bank and Trust, which is located just across the street; and the former state senator, Robert Mann. Contact with all of these people enables men who reside in the ghetto or who live by themselves in small Hyde Park apartments to feel connected with the larger society, by sharing public space or interacting with persons thought to be emblematic of it.

It is, of course, not merely the order of a wider world that men seek and find at Valois. They also discover the diversity of society, partially represented by the white citizens who belong to various social groups in the cafeteria. Werner Mandlebaum, for example, is one of a collectivity of white habitués, long-time residents of Hyde Park, who sometimes refer to themselves as old-timers. Werner lived with his mother until she was well into her eighties. When his demanding work schedule made it difficult for him to watch over her, his sister in North Dakota took her in. Although Werner often flew in his private plane to visit her on weekends, there was a gap left in his personal life. It was at this juncture that he began frequenting the cafeteria.

There he met Harry, a retired loan officer. The two men share a common interest in soy bean futures and pork bellies. When Harry became ill, Werner began driving him to and from Valois on a regular basis. He also supplied him with a collection of different caps from his cattle-buying trips. Werner gives Harry a call from his car telephone to let him know when he is on the way over. One can immediately identify them as members of the same circle because they both wear their caps there.

They usually join their cronies, Sebastian, Jim, and Gerald. Sebastian, a retired telegraph operator, worked for the army in a civilian capacity and retired two years ago. He is a long-time Hyde Parker who lived with his sick father for many years. A few months after his parent passed away, he began frequenting the cafeteria regularly. Sebastian's retired brother was the president of a large American toy company. When Sebastian retired, his brother began sending him five thousand dollars every six months with just one stipulation—that he spend the money and enjoy his retirement. Jim is a commodities trader in his late twenties—by far the youngest man in the otherwise aged group. Gerald, a semiretired dentist in his early sixties, has a practice outside the neighborhood. All these men are single, although Werner is sometimes accompanied by Frannie, a lady friend who is an esteemed member of the group. On Monday, Wednesday, and Thursday evenings the members of this clique meet at the cafeteria, often arriving at the same time.

Others who represent a wider society include students from the University of Chicago, especially on weekend mornings. But only those thought of as lifetime students are best known and recognized by the owners and other regulars. Some are young musicians and artists who are mistaken for students, but others are actual students—doctoral students who have been at the university for seven to ten years—and many are former Ph.D. candidates who have completed their course requirements but have never written the dissertation. Often the latter continue to study on their own while sitting in on occasional lectures, but never return to the university in any formal way.

Many of these men and women are thought by other students to be among the brighter and more intellectually serious members of the university community, despite their waywardness. They circulate freely within their large group and are open to discussions with a wide range of patrons. Some of the older regulars find the thought of making a career of remaining in school offensive, but black men like Ozzie sometimes praise the lifetime students for their interest in blues and other aspects of black culture: "The white students that come here, especially at night, are the ones who rebel against what the university tells them about the neighborhood. You see them around here. I also see some of them on Forty-seventh Street. I see them in the ghetto, way over on Forty-seventh, near Prairie. A lot of them go over there and listen to the blues. They get fed up with this racial attitude that they hear."

All of these groups, and the Greek owners, are equally a part of the life of Valois, and the black regulars consequently find it especially possible there to enter into a relationship with the other elements of a diverse society. Gratification from contact with the wider world is not usually derived only through interaction with its representatives, but more often by simple co-presence and people-watching. Smokey, for example, is a portly man of dark complexion who comes to the restaurant every night at about eight o'clock. He is one of the few regulars who owns his own business establishment, a candy store not far from the restaurant. Smoking a long cigar with obvious satisfaction, he usually sits by himself. From his seat, he can see everyone who comes into the restaurant. Most of the time he keeps to himself, although now and then he will look up and nod or mumble to someone he has seen in Valois for many years. He acknowledges that, although a loner, he enjoys being "in public." Men speak of being in public as being "in an environment." There are many people-watchers like Smokey, who derive an intense satisfaction from the mere co-presence of members of the wider society, even if they never come to know those people intimately.

It seems that a prerequisite for centering one's life in a public place like the restaurant is a deep and penetrating interest in others—not only the individuals that one meets, but those one merely notices from day to day. Many of the men, like Smokey, claim to be observers: "I sit by myself because I'm a loner. But I calculate everybody that I see. When I first saw you I calculated you. When a person walks in Valois, I'm automatically watching, and listening. I like to watch how they walk. That tells me something about a person. Not many people know that. You can tell a whole lot about a person by the way he walks. You can tell a whole lot about a person without ever meeting him. You seemed like one of those University of Chicago types. . . . You have to have a trained eye. You have to know what to look for. How they hold their head. How they talk. It's body language. And it tells you about a person. When I walk in Valois, I take a big glance around and I automatically get a big picture. Just by looking at the people here, I know all of them."

In such an environment, even those habitués who do not join the restaurant's established social groups cannot long maintain their anonymity. To the people-watchers, they become known, if not by name, by nicknames associated with salient characteristics such as physique or clothing. People-watching is especially satisfying at Valois because so many of the cafeteria's regulars are eccentrics. One such person is the black man in the pink suit, who came to the cafeteria at least twice each day before he left it in a rage and started eating at Wendy's instead. Every noon he would emerge from the Hyde Park Arms Hotel, one block from the restaurant. At eighty, clad in garish outfits and chunky costume jewelry, he was the kind of character who made people-watching at Valois effortless. Ever since he had a stroke, the walk to the cafeteria had become slow and painful for him. Now, when he holds up traffic by crossing the street, he is assaulted by a torrent of honks. Mindful yet undaunted, the old man laboriously makes his way to the other curb.

The man in the pink suit has a routine, still known to Slim and the other black Valois regulars who regard him as worthy of their attention. It begins at night in the lice-infested room that he rents at the transient hotel. He sits up until the small hours with a bottle of "Anything Goes" by his side and the television blasting, explaining to other lodgers down the hall, "I need my noise." Falling into a deep sleep is never easy. When it finally hits him—naturally or induced by pills—it is like his very own vision of death: He is gone. No worries. No debt. No hot. No cold. It is a release from living. And then by noon, when he comes down to the street to take his walk to eat, he has had his eight hours.

"I believe these will be my last days on earth. Is there anything worse than being dead?" he once asked a table of familiar black patrons upon entering the cafeteria.

"Being dead broke," called out a friend named Horace. The room echoed with the hearty laughter that often occurred when he entered in the old days, and he made his way, cane in hand, down to the counter to pick up a cup of coffee. Not everyone here respected this audacious man. Some were embarrassed to be associated with his showy style and they still say he is too eager for their attention. But inside the restaurant men like Slim—men who count—could sometimes find pleasure in his company.

The black regulars form an inner circle at Valois and the man in the pink suit, even as he eats at Wendy's, still stands at its edge. He is representative of many patrons, black and white, who are labeled "characters" by others and are indeed valued for their eccentricities. Many of these individuals have probably become odd as a consequence of solitary living. Conventional patrons derive satisfaction from being in the presence of these odd members of their society, even if that merely means watching them. This gratification can come from observing members of one's own primordial community, such as the man in the pink suit. But the significant pleasure of people-watching is to study members of the wider society who are different and try to explain and categorize them.

For the black regulars, an ability to understand what one sees of that world is sometimes a source of pride. It takes a trained eye to know what is really going on. Ozzie, who like Smokey, often sits alone, shows a similar pride in his ability to take in the scene around him: "I have studied psychology. So when I come to Valois I am just putting my theory to practice. I may not talk to people, but I don't have to talk to someone to know them. I studied all that stuff. You know, communication and all that sort of thing. At Valois you get all different kinds of personalities. You can tell about them by watching the way they eat, or talk, or walk. No amount of teaching will tell you this. But the theory helps. I can't help it if I've had sociological and psychological training. I can't help but see things that most people do not notice."

Officer Murphy says that he has done in-depth studies of most of the people who come into the cafeteria: "I say to myself, 'Murphy, what makes that man like that?' I'm a nosey person and I like to come to some solution as to how they got that way. My mind is like a computer. I'm always analyzing people. I'm trying to see where they're coming from, where they're going. If there is a possibility that I can get inside that little bubble that they have on top of their neck, I want to, and 99.9 percent of the time I can do it without ever meeting them."

The cafeteria is frequented by many people who are ostensibly uninvolved, but who nevertheless have the satisfaction of participating in their society. They are comfortable when they are sitting alone, as long as they are "among people," "in public," "in an environment."

Social life in the cafeteria is not typical of the wider society in that there is sometimes an almost total absence of women there. But a compelling feature of life at Valois is that, for these men, the wider society is embodied there in fundamental ways.

Sociability is not simply a precarious, artificial contrivance of human beings muting uncomfortable dimensions of stratification. More important, cafeteria life offers its regulars the opportunity to participate in the reality of the wider world itself. For here is one microcosm of society existing in its natural, objective form—an embodiment of power, cultural diversity, and behavioral expectations.

CHAPTER

7

A Higher Self

Human beings desire to participate in a world that validates their own image of self-worth. What is it about Valois, and especially the larger society, that confers a sense of respectability upon the black regulars?

Though these men still have great confidence in their own notions of "right" and "wrong," they sense also that the climate of opinion has turned, irresistibly, against whatever is correct. They are sensitive to their separateness when behaving in accordance with specific ideas of moral worth. Many of the black regulars no longer feel sufficiently comfortable in the ghetto to engage in the type of interaction that once predominated there. They feel an intense desire to rise above what they sometimes term the "negativity" of the streets, the moral isolation inherent in ghetto life. When they speak of the desire to escape from the lower depths in which they find themselves submerged, they mean they want to make contact with a world that is appropriate to their own sense of moral worth, one that represents greater order. To begin to understand the intensity of their moral isolation, it is important to again take note of how they feel about ghetto conditions.

Willie was sitting at one table while Elvin was sitting with me nearby.

While I was reading the paper, Elvin began describing conditions in the slum a few blocks away.

"Over there I will be violated," Willie chimed in. "It levels my nerves to come out here because nobody is gonna mess with you on Fifty-third Street."

Elvin went on to talk about what a violent country America had become. "If there was a good murder in a show we used to say, 'That actor really knows how to die good.' Now movies show so much blood that it doesn't take any talent to die."

The men laughed and joked, but beneath their jovial appearance was a sad acceptance of conditions.

Willie reminisced: "At that time you could sleep out there on a box and nobody would bother you. Try it now and it will be an eternal sleep."

Willie was referring to conditions on the other side of Cottage Grove Avenue, where many of the men in the restaurant used to live or still do. Throughout the conversation I had continued reading my newspaper. When I looked up, Willie's eyes met mine. Cocking his head back, he interrupted himself: "As long as you are my friend, Mitch, don't accept nothing over there. Don't go over there unless you have police and bodyguards with you."

I told Willie and Elvin not to worry, that I'd be afraid to walk around by myself. "I'm white and I'm not known in the neighborhood, but what do you have to worry about?"

"It don't make no difference," Willie responded vehemently. "They looking at your pocket. They don't give a damn if you black or white. If they think you got some money and you're black, you're just a black ass gone."

What is it about Valois that encourages the black regulars to participate in a group life which helps them "rise above" what they perceive as the low level of morality in the ghetto? Participation in the collectivity at Valois fosters a consciousness of oneself as an elevated human being, a person who has it within him, by virtue of demeanor and values, to be better than the sordid environment outside its doors. An activity as simple as "intelligent discussion" often suffices to make a man feel that he is engaging in conduct that signifies his assimilation into society.

Horace sat at my table and talked about some people near

his apartment on Forty-seventh Street who had been bothering him with their music.

"I told them to pick up their fucking bottles and to take their big musical briefcases away from my window."

This had been a continuing problem for Horace.

"That's the difference between the people on Forty-seventh Street and the guys here at Valois. Here people talk to each other. They listen to each other. They discuss the political situation in Chicago. They seem to be on an intellectual level. They seem to have an ability to sit and talk with anyone who's available. They seem to have the ability to talk things out."

To be intellectual is to talk about the serious things—like politics, religion, history, current events, and geography—that respectable members of society discuss. It is to speak and listen in a well-mannered way that in itself testifies to and validates an established sense of self-worth. For men who say they are immersed in a world where intelligent discussion is not readily found, there is a particular need to participate in a social world that affords the opportunity. Valois can meet that need.

Drake told me he had heard I was writing a novel about Valois. I told him that it wasn't a novel but, rather, a true story about the restaurant. Cornelius started telling me about the history of Valois, as men sometimes had when I mentioned that I was writing about the restaurant. Since most of my fieldwork had already been completed and I was no longer concerned about influencing the men to think about things that wouldn't normally have been on their minds, I interrupted him to explain that I wasn't interested in the history of the restaurant, so much as in why men came there.

Leroy, who had been sitting at the next table, turned toward us and said, "I'll tell you why everyone comes down to Valois. It is to escape from the realities of dealing with people outside of the cafeteria. Here it's like a separate world."

On another occasion, Horace, the articulate hairdresser, told me, "Valois is a place where I can relax. I get away from the negativity that you have on Forty-seventh Street. You find that every person on the corner is a whiskey head or a dope addict.

You see the depression. You see the person that you yourself don't want to be. And it hurts you that you have to pass through it. You don't want to consider yourself divorced from it, but you have to look at it and you don't want to accept it either. Where I live, it's cocaine city all day. They can hardly pay their rent. But that's what they do down on Forty-seventh Street. The depression is relieved when I come to a place like this. Valois is like a breath of fresh air. You see a level of person you can aspire to be. Where I live, a man just got shot in the head. I only associate with one man over there and he comes to Valois to escape."

As more and more of the regulars came to know that I had been writing about the restaurant, comments like these became very common. Officer Wilkens told me, "Most of the people who come here are broad-minded. It's a place where people can call you a honky or a nigger. It's just a brush-off. It's not a racial confrontation. It's a freeloading place. You can shoot as much shit as you want to and you don't have to worry about none of it getting in your face."

Social life at the cafeteria functions to bring about a conception of the collectivity as a means to the possession of higher self-worth. For a man to participate in an intelligent discussion with others is to be aware that he has a part of those ideas. What is true of them is true of him.[1]

This is not to suggest that the self-worth of black regulars is realized only through processes of social interaction in the restaurant. Such a view would miss an important dimension of these men—that they have strong characters, essentially formed in their youth and reinforced both by the working world and the ascetic demands of their own culture. It is important to distinguish between two images: a man's image of his own worth as an individual, independent of its relationship to the wider society, and his image of himself as a participant in the wider society.

The distinction has particular meaning for our discussion. Whereas the black cafeteria man does not "realize" who he is through processes of interaction, his participation in society does foster a consciousness of himself as an elevated person, one who carries within himself what is true and worthwhile about ideas and modes of conduct that are the foundation of life at Valois. These two images can exist simultaneously, but while the first is permanent and enduring, the second needs to be reinforced and renewed from time to time. The first image is routine and ordinary—the person that one has always been, the self-esteem with which he lives from day to day. The second image manifests itself in an infrequent, intense, and concentrated way. This is the perception of self-worth sometimes reawakened through participation in society.

The way in which society confers respectability upon ghetto dwellers is best understood through the metaphor of the relationship between charismatic and ordinary experience.[2] One example of this functional relationship can be seen in the way that certain friendships between blacks and whites at Valois bring about a self-image of the black participant as a person of higher worthiness than the conditions in which he normally finds himself submerged can testify to. The act of engaging in meaningful relationships with "white folks" brings more vividly into the minds of some regulars images of themselves which they can only infrequently experience in other contexts.

During my years at the cafeteria, Chicago was a city that had grown accustomed to being described in the national and local press as "racially polarized." The election of a black as mayor, the ensuing battles between that mayor, Harold Washington, and white aldermen for control of the city council, had been described by the media as symbolic of racial tensions between blacks and whites at all levels in the city. Those who wrote about these tensions in the daily press or reported them on television would claim that they were bringing the madness of the streets to life in print or on the screen. One sensitive and respected young moderate black reporter for the *Chicago Tribune* published an article in the *Washington Post* that typified the way the Chicago media were depicting race relations for the citizens of their own city. The *Post* article, "How Chicago Taught Me to Hate Whites," chronicled in a Baldwinesque way the reporter's personal bitterness toward her own "liberal" white friends for the "evilness" of white ethnics who opposed Mayor Washington. On the subject of racial tension in Chicago, she wrote: "Even black and white secretaries in City Hall are not speaking to each other. . . . In the police stations, reports were whispered about fights between long-time black and white squad car partners."[3]

Articles and television reports like this one were very common during my years as a patron at Valois. As a result, the image of the city in the minds of many of its inhabitants was that of a battleground between the races. Of course, most black and white secretaries in the city did not work at City Hall, and it certainly was not the case that people of different races had, en masse, stopped talking to one another. The racial tensions that existed in City Hall or inside the premises of the *Tribune* were hardly representative of what went on in the rest of Chicago. But a combination of blacks and whites who had amicable relations with one another, blacks who hardly ever saw whites, and whites who hardly ever saw blacks were being told that they were living in a state of conflict.

These were not the kinds of images that made the citizens of the city, black or white, feel good about themselves. At Valois, the regulars had the means to keep it all in perspective. They derived obvious satisfaction from their positive and meaningful contact with whites in the restaurant. Racial coexistence was a fact. As Wilkens said to me: "Some black people feel a little need to see people who are white. It's like letting off a little steam. You read something in the newspaper about race relations and you want to get a review of what the persons who are supposed to be saying this about them are really saying. And here they feel they can express their opinion."

"Maybe some blacks can't get along with whites, but I certainly can," Horace, the hairdresser, once told me as we discussed the political situation in Chicago, "I have both black friends and white friends at Valois." For a man who is accustomed to hearing from the news media that he is in a state of daily conflict with whites, positive contact with a few white people can be very gratifying, in the same way that meaningful contact with black people is satisfying to whites who are similarly besieged.

Although all of the black regulars were very proud of Mayor Washington, many of them took equal pride in their own ability to get along with those whom the press suggested were represented by Washington's foes. On one occasion I asked Horace what it was that he liked so much about Valois. He began by telling me that he came because of the food, but he went on to say, "Then, of course, I get a chance to associate with whites on a social level. I can come to Valois and for a few minutes I can pretend that I am in a nonracist world. Valois is a special place on the planet earth. It is the only place that I have this much unity going on in my life."

Horace found the words to express the relationship that exists between two different images of self-worth. He lives and works in the ghetto. According to what the man on the television says, he has good reason to believe that Chicago is racially polarized. Such conditions are deeply felt and regretted by many sensitive people, and Horace is one of these. When he suggests that Valois is the only place where there is such "unity going on" in his life, he recognizes that at the restaurant he is part of something that manifests itself in an intense and concentrated form only in that setting. Like many—but certainly not all—older blacks who were raised in a racist society, Horace has learned not to place too much faith in his relationships with whites; when he refers to such associations, he explicitly recognizes that he must pretend that he is in a nonracist world. When he goes to the restaurant, he is gratified by the interaction that takes place—even if there is a make-believe element to the whole situation.[4] The image that he has of himself as a unit separate from the collectivity is that of a man who, on a day-to-day basis, knows that he is worthy yet is in a state of conflict with white people. By contrast, the image that he has of himself as a participant in the collectivity fosters a consciousness of his own moral worth as higher than the enduring, permanent core of a person he lives with from day to day.

Horace knows that he and the black men he hangs out with don't fit the stereotyped images that many whites have of black people, and he finds it gratifying to be recognized as somehow different from the stereotype: "It used to be that the older, well-to-do white guys who wear caps didn't associate with me. I would sit down with them and they would find some reason to get up and leave. Now those men accept the fact that I am not the ordinary black guy. I feel their evaluation of what the black man is is stereotyped. They have a picture of what a black man is in their mind and that is not necessarily the way it is. But they see me as something different." A man's self-image as a participant in group life at Valois reawakens a consciousness of himself as elevated above the degradation of everyday "racial polarization."

It is, of course, not only positive interaction with white patrons that serves to make these black men feel that they have risen to a higher level of worthiness. Even more important to the realization of self-images of respectability at Valois is the fact that the restaurant embodies some of those ineffable qualities that once permeated life in the old ghetto just a few blocks away. Old-fashioned food with natural ingredients, a meeting place that conjures up both an old barbership and an old neighborhood, and frequent discussion of beliefs and opinions that originated in the old black community—all serve to remind a man of his former participation in a community that, in fundamental ways, molded his patterns of belief and conduct, creating the human being that he was to become.

Although they are essential to his images of self-worth, these dimensions of himself easily lose vividness as he conducts his affairs in a state of perceived moral isolation that seems to bear no relationship to that former life. Like a charismatic experience, the image of his respectability cannot be maintained in an intense and concentrated form by the uninspired actions of daily life. No human being is constantly infused with the state of mind of his highest morality. The image of oneself living in accordance with the pattern of values inherent in the concept of respectability is, in this particular case, only reawakened intermittently by participation in those situations which are most fundamental to a man's self-worth. For a man of this kind, these interactions indicate something about the kind of person that he objectively is—not, however, in the sense of which group he fits into or how the group or category he belongs to contrasts with other groups. In this case, the kind of person that he conceives himself to be is ultimately indicative of a relationship between himself and himself. It is the relationship between the image of self-worth with which he lives from day to day and the perception of respectability that derives from participation in the larger society embodied at Valois.

PART

4

You're White, He's Black, I'm a Sociologist: Who's Innocent?

CHAPTER

8

The Underclass and the Middle Class

Contemporary discussions of urban poverty in sociology and
journalism are characterized by the assumption that the separation between middle and upper working-class blacks and the
ghettos is tantamount to the separation between the black community and its own moral base. One poignant example of this
manifested itself in an ABC News documentary entitled "Black
in White America."[1] On this occasion, the president of ABC
News invited an all-black unit of producers and correspondents
to make a documentary for prime-time viewing. Here was an
opportunity for blacks with complete editorial control to deter-
mine how they themselves would portray the experience of
being black in a white society. The program's black producer
hoped to break new ground by showing "for the first time not
just one aspect of black America, but a variety of black Americans, from various walks of life." One of the program's correspondents began by telling the nationwide audience: "They are
people you don't normally see or hear on television . . . they
are people that represent the great diversity that is black life in
this country." But even with such intentions, this all-black editorial unit could not transcend the most common stereotypes of
the black community as it focused completely on those blacks
who were either members of the underclass or the relatively
prospering black middle class. According to the black anchor-
man, there are the blacks who have made it and those who

haven't. The first segment of the program therefore focused on "real life versions of the Cosby Show," people "struggling to maintain their black identity in a world that doesn't always value it." The viewer was introduced to a family that lives in a half-million dollar home, "not because they wanted to live with whites, but because they couldn't find the house they wanted in a black neighborhood." The second segment of the program focused on the underclass, with typical references to the idea that drugs are shipped to the ghettos in a conspiracy to commit genocide against black people. A third segment focused on a group of former black fighter pilots, notable for their distinctiveness. In their failure to focus on the majority of respectable poor ghetto dwellers in a program that was devoted to representing the "variety" of black America, one had the distinct impression that these black writers were sharply out of touch with their own population.

A similar tendency was apparent in a project no less substantial conducted by *Newsweek*.[2] In 1987, the magazine sent a team of its black reporters to a Chicago housing project, collecting the stories of men who were known to one of the reporters, who had himself grown up in the projects before attending an elite boarding school in the East. In a preface to the special issue, published under the title "Brothers," the magazine's editor-in-chief wrote, "While no single story can sum up an entire community, we believe this special report goes far beyond all the stereotypes and the statistics to tell in important detail what it's like to grow up black and poor in America." The ten men who were selected for coverage in the story were (1) a killer, drug dealer, and heroin user; (2) a former heroin user and high school dropout who now worked at a blue-collar job; (3) a former wife beater who kept a step ahead of the bill collectors; (4) a failed professional basketball player who became a drug dealer; (5) a high school dropout, formerly addicted to heroin, cocaine, and diet pills, now a Jehovah's Witness; (6) a high school dropout and former gang member; (7) a former heroin user who spent a year in federal prison; (8) a dropout from Northwestern University who "had a chance but didn't take it," lived off women and abused drugs, and hadn't worked in seven years; (9) a middle-class beneficiary of affirmative action; and (10) a black nationalist yuppie. Many readers undoubtedly concluded that *Newsweek's* choices reflected empirical reality; that those who grow up in the projects are either unstable blacks or middle-class examples of affirmative action. Not a single man among the twelve who grew up in the projects was a stable working-class or working-poor man. Certainly, if the magazine could track down those who were now living in middle-class neighborhoods, it is not inconceivable that some of those stable working men who had migrated to neighboring working-class districts or who still lived in the projects could also be included. The report, which received widespread attention and acclaim, ironically misled the American public in representing itself as going "far beyond all the stereotypes" while actually reinforcing the most common stereotypes of black men.

The question of whether the black reporters from ABC News and *Newsweek* were out of touch with their own population is not so simple. What their cliché-ridden documentaries actually illustrate is the extent to which the crude distinction between underclass and middle class has become part of the stereotype of the black population.[3] More important, this stereotype has been accepted by blacks—like these reporters—and become part of the black experience itself. Thus, even an entirely black unit of television journalists conceived of its community in such terms, thereby excluding the vast majority of ordinary, working blacks from their presentation of the "variety" of the black population.

In the popular imagination influenced by these sociological and journalistic accounts, only white society has a complete class structure that includes "respectable" lower classes that work.[4] The vast majority of men at Valois are members of the black working and working-poor classes by virtue of occupation, lifestyle, and values—although a casual observer might see a few solidly middle-class blacks like Earl and mistake the others for middle class as well. This is a function of the myopia of sociological class analysis as applied to the black population, resulting in such crude distinctions that those who are not "riff-raff" are thought to be middle class. The prevalent dichotomy between middle class and underclass has resulted in a tendency to associate any "respectable" behavioral characteristics in black people with a middle-class orientation. Men like the regulars at Valois, who like other members of society are to be sure influenced in some measure by such reports, are themselves prone to talk about the black population in terms of these crude distinctions. They do so as if they themselves are somehow insignificant or exist outside the mass that makes a difference. The prevalent imagery of the black class structure renders the most effective agents of social control in the black community irrelevant in the debate over the future of their own people.

In recent years, the most prominent explanation for ghetto problems has emphasized the significance of increased concentrations of poverty within certain already poor neighborhoods as a result of the economic transformation of the city. In the key work on this subject, *The Truly Disadvantaged*, William Julius Wilson focused on the exodus of large numbers of working and middle-class blacks from the ghettos, which he believes magnifies the "social isolation" of poor blacks from mainstream values and behavioral patterns. His argument consists of two parts: first, residential segregation of the poor has increased; second, the effects of this residential segregation in terms of a decline of role models and neighborhood institutions has been devastating to the inner city. With reference to the second part of his argument, Wilson wrote,

A perceptive ghetto youngster in a neighborhood that includes a good number of working and professional families may observe increasing joblessness and idleness but he will also witness many individuals regularly going to and from work; he may sense an increase in school dropouts but he can also see a connection between education and meaningful employment; he may detect a growth in single-parent families, but he will also be aware of the presence of many married-couple families; he may notice an increase in welfare dependency, but he can also see a significant number of families that are not on welfare; and he may be cognizant of an increase in crime, but he can recognize that many residents in his neighborhood are not involved in criminal activity.[5]

Wilson's hypotheses set the agenda for poverty research in the 1980s and 1990s. Wilson used census data to show that poverty was becoming more concentrated within certain zones of the city. Within academic circles, serious debate focused on the extent to which residential segregation of the poor was increasing.[6] By the beginning of the 1990s, there were numerous demographic studies of poverty concentration, but only a scattering of conflicting studies indicating how it might matter that poverty was more concentrated. There was little serious discussion of Wilson's assertions about the significance of middle-class role models. There was a general belief that middle-class people who left the inner city had been significant to urban neighborhoods, but the lack of discussion about the meaning of the role model concept was matched by little evidence.[7] As a consequence, theorizing by sociologists and journalists about the effects of this segregation in terms of a decline of mainstream patterns of norms and behavior only repeated contemporary folklore.

One significant effort to explain the meaning of this demographic transition can be found in Elijah Anderson's *Streetwise*, an ethnographic study that attempts to use Wilson's demographic theory to give order to its wide range of data and observations. Attempting to comprehend what has been lost by the middle-class departure, Anderson argues that middle-class (and upper working-class) ghetto dwellers in Philadelphia "served the black community well as visible, concrete symbols of *success* and *moral value*, living examples of the fruits of *hard work, perseverance, decency,* and *propriety*" (p. 58; emphasis mine). In using these words and phrases to explain the specific contribution of these groups to the ghetto, Anderson distinguishes between the ghetto dwellers who have departed and those who have been left behind. He argues that the people who departed "were effective, meaningful role models, lending the community a certain moral integrity" (p. 59). The tendency to explain what has been lost to the ghettos by using such phrases to describe middle-class blacks (and even working-class blacks with better jobs) implies that the majority of ghetto dwellers who work at low-wage jobs do not have these moral characteristics.

Scholars like Wilson and Anderson have themselves been prominent in correctly calling attention to the fact that the Reagan economic boom consisted of the expansion of numerous low-wage jobs, rather than factory positions that pay better. Where in this image of a ghetto devoid of people who lend the ghetto moral integrity is this new class of occupants of low-wage jobs? When scholars use words like "perseverance" and "decency" to explain the significance of the role model concept, and to distinguish middle-class blacks from blacks with low-wage jobs, one begins to wish the large amount of census research on the departure of the middle class had occurred in a richer theoretical context. With such clichés there has emerged in scholarly literature an image of the mainstream ghetto population that accords with generally accepted stereotypes rather than evidence. Phrases like "moral value" and "decency" do not accurately distinguish the character of the blacks who have departed from the ones who are left behind.

The dominant view is that people in the higher social classes, representing the different culture of the wider society, can be effective agents in transforming values in the ghetto. But there is good reason to be skeptical of this hypothesis. Part of the problem with the role model explanation is that it follows from the sociological discipline's oversimplified images of the urban ghettos as significantly cut off from the rest of American society. Wilson introduced the term "social isolation" to describe the lack of ghetto contact with mainstream culture, and it has since been picked up by the mass media. But, as Christopher Jencks has illustrated, the idea fails to acknowledge the extent to which the problems of ghetto life reflect broader trends in the wider society.[8] What distinguishes the poor from other members of society is not that they are isolated from mainstream values, but that they do not have the standard of living to buffer them from the destructive effects of the permissiveness, freedom, and spontaneity of American life. Many pathological social trends in the ghetto are more concentrated reflections of life in the wider society. As Gerald Suttles argues, "We must dig more into the white community, especially its more liberal reaches, to see how its rhetoric of emancipation is destructive in both the black and white community."[9]

When the types of people most commonly referred to as black role models are basketball stars who father babies out of wedlock, the higher classes have less to offer in the way of superior values than one might have hoped. When Los Angeles Laker cocaptain James Worthy, a married man, is arrested on charges of solicitation of prostitution, does not the ovation he receives from mostly white audiences immediately after that event reflect the fact that the wider society is enmeshed in the same confusion over traditional values? Certainly these crowds would feel no compunction about booing or hissing a player who played badly. And what about the remarks of another so-called role model, Magic Johnson, when he defends his teammate saying, "I don't know what happened. . . . Doesn't matter what happened . . . James came out and helped us get the win."[10] The poorest and most estranged members of society are not likely to take seriously cultural lessons from white society or from the black middle and upper classes, especially when these references are themselves caught up in those webs of conflicting value orientations that include permissive attitudes toward teenage sex, childbearing out of wedlock, adultery, and divorce that are prevalent in the wider society.

In addition to assuming that ghetto dwellers are significantly cut off from the wider society and that the wider society possesses superior values, role model notions also assume that poor people will imitate the values of the middle classes, despite the fact that they don't have similar resources. The saying

"Middle-class morality is all very well if you can afford it" has not been taken seriously by sociologists. Yet, the best evidence for the view that opportunity is crucial to the efficacy of role models is Anderson's own description of a stratum of older black men whom he calls "old heads." Like Slim and his sitting buddies at Valois, these are working-class people who embody traditional values in the black community. According to Anderson, "Traditionally the 'old head' was a man of stable means who believed in hard work, family life, and the church. He was an aggressive agent of the wider society whose acknowledged role was to teach, support, encourage, and in effect socialize young men to meet their responsibilities regarding work, family, the law, and common decency" (p. 3). Anderson's book, *Streetwise*, is on one level a brilliant description of the decline of these men within the ghettos and a meditation on their seeming irrelevance in the face of the decline of industry and new lessons the young learn from drug dealers. Anderson comments, "The youths mock and patronize the old heads who do remain [in the community] for not understanding 'the way the world really works' " (p. 242).

Anderson's *Streetwise* can be read as a meditation on the moral isolation of respectable citizens. Had his attempt to delineate the parameters and significance of this stratum of men within the ghetto stood on its own, it might have served as a brilliant corrective to the pervasive oversimplification of the ghetto class structure. Instead, in some other parts of his book, Anderson tries to relate the deterioration of the ghetto to Wilson's demographic thesis about the disappearance of middle- and working-class ghetto dwellers. If traditional working-class role models in the ghetto have so declined in prestige, as Anderson claims, one is left to question the demographic assumption regarding the significance of the supposed loss of middle-class role models. Why, if the lessons of the working-class old heads are ignored, would the lessons of the middle class be taken seriously? There is actually no real contradiction, but the answer can lead us to a more differentiated conception of the role model. If the underclass ignores working-class role models who are most likely to provide entry into relevant job networks, we need to know why they would pay any more heed to middle-class role models. Is it simply because they are richer?

One evocative way that scholars point out the significance of the middle class is to romanticize it. They draw comparisons with an earlier time when the ghetto supposedly had greater class integration. Anderson contrasts prior ghettos to contemporary black neighborhoods: "In the past," he writes, "blacks of various social classes lived side by side in segregated Northton, a 'Negro' section of the city. They shared racially separate neighborhood institutions, including churches, schools, barber shops, and even liquor stores and taverns" (p. 58). Statements like these are intended to show that the old ghetto has changed dramatically by the sudden exodus of the population of middle- and working-class people. "Because of their presence and the honor accorded them, there was more cohesion among individuals and the various classes of the black community than is generally seen today," writes Anderson (pp. 58–59).

However, these images of the old-time black ghettos are rooted less in empirical evidence than in anecdotes and nostalgia. The particular way in which the working and lower classes relied upon the middle classes is never articulated and the concept of cohesion, though evocative, does not provide explanation. Anderson's anecdotal descriptions of Philadelphia's past in *Streetwise*[11] do not make reference to the best-detailed survey, conducted by DuBois around the turn of the century, which presents little evidence to support such notions. In *The Philadelphia Negro* DuBois gives no grounds for thinking that "the middle classes and those above" lived alongside the lowest classes. Even when they were in physical proximity, he makes clear that the classes that have declined as vital members of the ghetto never did have much to do with the lower elements:

They are not the leaders or the ideal-makers of their own group in thought, work, or morals. They teach the masses to a very small extent, mingle with them but little, do not largely hire their labor. Instead then of social classes held together by strong ties of mutual interest, we have in the case of the Negroes, classes who have much to keep them apart, and only community of blood and color prejudice to bind them together. If the Negroes were by themselves, either a strong aristocratic system or a dictatorship would for the present prevail. With, however, democracy thus prematurely thrust upon them, the first impulse of the best, the wisest and the richest is to segregate themselves from the mass.[12]

Although the belief that there was significant interaction among various social classes in the old-time ghettos is usually only supported by anecdotes, it is a substantial component of the attempt to understand urban deterioration as a function of the decline of available role models.[13] Sociologists fail to acknowledge the historical strength of the black working and lower working classes, creating the impression that without middle-class and even upper working-class respectability the black community is devoid of its moral base. Thus, social theory about urban poverty fails to recognize that the working poor are moral beings that can provide their own role models, at least on moral grounds.

This is not to say that middle-class people have little significance to the ghettos. But it is not necessary to demean the black working classes or to create a sensational picture of ghetto life to suggest that middle-class role models are crucial to these communities.[14] It is certainly not appropriate, in an effort to explain the significance of the supposed middle-class exodus, to use words like "honesty" and "perseverance" to distinguish the departing middle classes from those left behind. Such use merely replicates the racism of the larger society in the guise of "theory." It certainly makes sense that the presence of middle-class people provides inspiration to ghetto dwellers that others like themselves can advance in American society. No less sensible, though not sufficiently explored, is the notion that middle-class people can serve as powerful bulwarks to the extent that the ghettos are enmeshed in conflicts among various forms of authority.

In his classic essay, "Charisma, Order, and Status," Edward Shils has written of the need of human beings to "locate themselves and connect themselves with a larger order that gives meaning to discrete and otherwise meaningless events. . . . In no society can the problem of the larger order be avoided entirely."[15] Who gains the authority to interpret experience for the great masses, to enunciate propositions that will serve to guide life as principles? Like the wider society, but even more so, the ghettos are typified by tremendous competition among different bases of authority. In communities where drug dealers and gang leaders and some rap musicians compete with the churches, the schools, and working-class values for the attention of formative minds, it is no surprise that traditional bases of authority feel threatened.

Every society is constituted of its creators and its maintainers. The working classes are maintainers; they reproduce society through the enactment of recurrent processes in the framework of established institutions. Drug dealers and gang leaders are creators of new structures and symbolic patterns which depart from the others. Even rap musicians, though often correctly conceived as vehicles of self-definition and the embodiment of the black oral tradition and sometimes of positive values, usually work outside the locus of institutions like the church and the school, disrupting traditional authority with messages celebrating materialism, reckless spontaneity, and sexual freedom. All due exceptions aside, much rap music legitimizes the most extreme forms of permissiveness, all of which function to distort the seemingly natural relation between ends and means and the working-class conception of value. In the face of the assault on traditional institutions, the ghettos cannot rely upon the simple maintainers of old structures—the working classes—to win the battle. They need the support of those who derive charisma from contact with the locus of the authority of society, those middle-class and professional people who are thought to be emblematic of authoritative institutional roles. The significance of the middle-class or professional person in the ghetto is conceived in much the same way as Shils's description of the reaction to a command or judgment enunciated by an incumbent at the higher levels of an organization:

> It is conceived as a "part" or as an emanation of the cosmos of commands and judgments at the center of which is a supremely authoritative principle or a supremely authoritative role incorporating that principle. The particular incumbent of the role . . . is perceived as the manifestation of a larger center of tremendous power.
>
> What the "subject" responds to is not just the specific declaration or order of the incumbent of the role . . . but the incumbent enveloped in the vague and powerful nimbus of the authority of the entire institution. It is a legitimacy constituted by sharing in the properties of the organization as a whole epitomized or symbolized in the powers concentrated at the peak. (p. 266)

Even among ghetto dwellers who reside far from the locus of institutional power, charisma is attributed to the incumbents of authority-exercising roles.[16] Shils writes that in order for the traditional social order to be legitimated, it must "not only give the impression of being coherent and continuous; it must also appear to be integrated with a transcendent moral order" (p. 266). As traditional bases of authority such as the church attempt to legitimate themselves without the help of the middle and professional classes (those who would provide the link between poverty conditions and mainstream lifestyles that lends coherence to an otherwise discrepant social structure), they seem weak when opposed to the competing powers of gang leaders, drug dealers, and even those nonconstructive rap musicians who stand at the peaks of new competing structures of authority which they have created and maintain. The recognition that the middle and professional classes embody a symbolic universe that derives its legitimacy from a more comprehensive legitimacy, closer to the source of greater earthly authority, is essential to comprehending what is missing from a community that lacks their presence.

The idea of the role model has long been a part of American sociological thought, but it has been used inappropriately in the debate over the future of the inner city. The concept of role model denotes a more limited identification with an individual in only one or a selected few of his or her roles.[17] The departure of middle-class and upper working-class people from the inner city described in demographic studies is more appropriately conceptualized as the departure of an entire constellation of values, not segmented roles. Indeed, this is what sociologists like Wilson usually mean when they speak of the middle-class departure, and it would therefore be more appropriate to speak of what sociologists once called reference individuals. In his classic essays on the reference group concept in the 1960s, Robert K. Merton wrote about them as people whose

> multiple roles are adopted for emulation rather than emulation remaining confined to the one role on the basis of which the initial psychological relationship was established. Just as roles can be segregated from one another in the course of social interaction, so they can be in the form of reference orientations. Emulation of a peer, a parent or a public figure may be usefully described as adoption of a role model. Or emulation may be extended to a wider array of behaviors and values of these persons who can then be described as reference individuals. (Pp. 356–57)

In the demographic studies of the inner city and the research influenced by them, the role model concept was bandied about with little precision as to what it meant. The explanation that argues for the significance of role models by declaring the poor devoid of "perseverance" and other moral qualities is a needless perpetuation of a damaging myth. Middle-class people are significant for the inspiration and coherence fostered by their presence in ghetto communities. But we need only reflect on the stories of Jackson and his receipts and of Slim and Bart, among many others, to recognize that the working poor and working classes are capable of providing moral references for themselves and for middle-class people as well.

As gatekeepers of the standard images of black life, many sociologists and journalists have abdicated their responsibility to look beyond folk images derived from public displays of indecency. They have portrayed the black community in terms of crude distinctions between the "respectable" black middle and upper working classes, now supposedly departed from the scene, and the black lumpenproletariat, that segment of black society popularly known as the "underclass."

Stable working-class and working-poor blacks are least visible to sociologists and journalists who move in and out of these neighborhoods at a quick pace, collecting information with cameras and tape recorders that makes sensational copy and serves to reinforce the existing stereotypes. Complex, subtle portraits of the black community do not make good sound bites on the evening news and require more time in the black milieu than the few hours or days spent by journalists, or even the extended months devoted by some social scientists and rare journalistic projects. Men like the black regulars at Valois who aspire to the standard of respectability have been left behind by these conventional, impatient treatments of their community; they do not fit into the sensational accounts which prevail in the images of black neighborhoods offered by social scientific accounts, television, and newspapers. The opportunity of social scientists and the mass media to make the "respectable" masses part of the "on-going perceived reality"[18] has been forgone.

CHAPTER

9

The Stereotype of Blacks in
Sociology and Journalism

Consider these fictitious quotations from an imaginary black sociologist who has conducted fieldwork among American Jews:

"The American status-symbol quest becomes an obsession in the Jewish community, where conspicuous consumption—the acquisition of the biggest cars and the flashiest clothes—sometimes takes precedence over adequate food and shelter."

"The inside trader is an ideal type representing an important value orientation for the Jew. If we are ever to understand what Jewish culture is all about, we had best view inside traders on Wall Street as culture heroes—integral parts of the whole—rather than as deviants or shadow figures."

Unfortunately, black scholars tend not to conduct sociological studies of white ethnic groups (as do white scholars of blacks), but one suspects that if books made such assertions as illustrated above about a white ethnic group—Jews are only an example—without clear and unambiguous evidence, they would have little chance of getting assigned in college classes to generations of students. If such books were assigned in sociology classes, there would probably be an outcry not unlike that heard when honest productions of Shakespeare's *Merchant of Venice* are considered for staging. Yet each of the above statements by our imaginary black sociologist parallels typical assertions made by black and white sociologists in works on the black male regarded as classics.

In a national bestseller, *The Content of Our Character,* Shelby Steele, an English professor, made some generalizations about the black underclass that were unsupported by any evidence beyond his observations of middle-class blacks. But in separate parts of his book, he spoke with great insight into the relationship between the quest for power and the assertion of innocence:

> The human animal almost never pursues power without first convincing himself that he is *entitled* to it. And this feeling of entitlement has its own precondition: to be entitled one must first believe in one's innocence, at least in the area where one wishes to be entitled. By innocence I mean a feeling of essential goodness in relation to others and, therefore, superiority to others. Our innocence always inflates us and deflates those we seek power over. Once inflated we are entitled; we are in fact licensed to go after the power our innocence tells us we deserve. In this sense, *innocence is power.* . . . Its only test is whether or not we can convince ourselves of it.[1]

Sociology, like many disciplines today, is constituted of some scholars who tend to function as politically correct stereotype guardians. They say, "You are guilty of carrying around an unenlightened, negative image of blacks. But you can depend upon me, in my innocence and enlightenment, to set you straight." Sociologists write books which advertise themselves as providing, to quote Lee Rainwater on the back of Ulf Hannerz's *Soulside*, a "more accurate and less stereotyped view of the lower-class black man's world."[2] An educated public has long relied on sociology, as it has relied on no other academic discipline, to refine its conception of the black population. Indeed, one of the great legacies of sociology since World War II is its collection of landmark field studies of the black population that include Drake and Cayton's *Black Metropolis*, Charles Keil's *Urban Blues*, Elliot Liebow's *Tally's Corner*, Lee Rainwater's *Behind Ghetto Walls*, Ulf Hannerz's *Soulside*, and Elijah Anderson's *A Place on the Corner* and *Streetwise*. As a body of work these books constitute one of the great achievements of American sociology during the past half-century, demonstrating the potential of empirical social science to build upon itself and foster self-understanding for the wider society.

In discussing the urban ethnographic tradition, I immediately recall how much more enlightened I felt after some of my own gross stereotypes about blacks were transcended through an encounter with these works. I think particularly of Elijah Anderson's *A Place on the Corner*, which examined a group of streetcorner men that most Americans would conceive as indecent. Anderson showed what a powerful tool ethnography can be as he broke down the stereotype of the corner men and demonstrated that among this group of seeming "no counts," the corner had a stratification system of its own that consisted of regular working men, winos, and hoodlums. Anderson's exploration of the concept of "decency" among the regularly employed men, and his analysis of the manner in which the respectable workers create the categories for winos and hoodlums on the street, served alongside Hannerz's *Soulside* and Drake and Cayton's *Black Metropolis* as an inspiration to me as I conducted my own fieldwork on the South Side of Chicago.

Yet after my own years of attempting to build closely upon these inspiring studies, I came to question whether the public influenced by such works has placed too much faith in them. The sociologist's success at conveying his or her "essential goodness in relation to others," most commonly by simply advertising that his or her books present a less stereotyped view of blacks, or by embracing a liberal political program, has afforded a license to make generalizations about the black population that are not supported by firm evidence. What is most surprising about these studies is that the elevation of innocence over evidence as an entitlement to generalize has not even led to a more positive image of blacks. Yet, because these books are written by scholars who so successfully establish their innocence, it has largely gone unnoticed that as a body of work they confirm inaccurate stereotypes that happen also to be demeaning. As we shall see, ethnographers have made an industry out of studying black men and making generalizations that would be regarded as unacceptable if they were made about white ethnic groups with as little evidence, or even if they were made by scholars who failed to establish their own "essential goodness in relation to others" so successfully.

I came to question whether even these works successfully fulfill the mission of breaking down conventional categories. Is there really a difference between the general image of blacks in popular opinion and in the most prominent works of sociology?

The esteem accorded the major studies illustrates the consensus among scholars and the public that sociology has brought its audience out of the Dark Ages in refining its understanding of poor blacks. This is well reflected in the words of a historian writing about sociological research on urban poverty:

> The method of ethnography contrasts vividly with quantitative studies of poverty. Its minimal contribution is the destruction of stereotypes; its signal achievement, in the work of its most able practitioners, is a portrait of the world from the vantage point of its subjects. The best ethnographies always break down conventional categories and reassemble the lived world of their subjects in the terms of their subjective experience.[3]

This analysis is typical. Ethnographic writing on the black population claims to render a more differentiated portrait of blacks than is found in other places. These books are therefore lauded as enlightening portraits, assigned to students enrolled in sociology courses on race and urban affairs, and pointed to as exemplars of the potentialities of qualitative social science. Over the past two decades they have been read by multitudes of young whites like myself, and even by young blacks who take African-American studies courses designed to promote self-understanding. The burden that falls upon these works is therefore very great. Generations of policymakers and students have now relied upon them for their images of black urban life.

One way to take stock of sociology's progress is to compare the view of blacks that emerges in literature and popular writing with the pictures painted by these scholars who have done ethnographic work in the ghettos. One image of blacks in the popular imagination is epitomized by Norman Mailer's description:

> The Negro has the simplest of alternatives: live a life of constant humility or ever-threatening danger. In such a pass where paranoia is as vital to survival as blood, the Negro had stayed alive and begun to grow by following the need of his body where he could. Knowing in the cells of his existence that life was war, nothing but war, the Negro (all exceptions admitted) could rarely afford the sophisticated inhibitions of civilization, and so he kept for his survival the art of the primitive, he lived in the enormous present, he subsisted for his Saturday night kicks, relinquishing the pleasures of the mind for the more obligatory pleasures of the body, and in his music he gave voice to the character and quality of his existence, to his rage and the infinite variations of joy, lust, languor, growl, cramp, pinch, scream and despair of his orgasm.[4]

Charles Keil's portrait in *Urban Blues*, a well-regarded sociological study of blues musicians, epitomizes the sociological view:

> The values usually associated with Protestantism—thrift, sobriety, "inner-directedness," strictly codified sexual behavior (better to marry than to burn), and a strong insistence on respectability—tend to be reversed in the Negro cultural framework. Preachers and elderly Negro women love to give these lip service, but that's usually as far as conventional Protestantism goes.[5]

> The American status-symbol quest becomes an obsession in the Negro community, where conspicuous consumption—the acquisition of the biggest cars and the flashiest clothes—sometimes takes precedence over adequate food and shelter. (Pp. 11–12)

The hustler (or underworld denizen) and the entertainer
are ideal types representing two important value orientations for the lower-class Negro and need not be distin-
guished from the lower class as a whole. . . . If we are
ever to understand what urban Negro culture is all about,
we had best view entertainers and hustlers as culture heroes—integral parts of the whole—rather than as deviants or shadow figures. (P. 20)

This statement about the black community as a whole is derived from a study of a limited group of blues musicians. Yet, as
the stories of Slim and his sitting buddies unfolded before my
eyes in the cafeteria, I began to question the ways in which
"enlightened" books of this kind, written by progressive scholars, give significant support to popular images like Mailer's. Although it is not incorrect to say that the greatest ethnographies
have challenged many inaccurate stereotypes, one should not
rely too greatly upon ethnography for an enlightened image,
for these works concomitantly foster many of the same inaccurate images of blacks that existed for members of the general
public before they read the accounts. The limited range of
these accounts goes unnoticed as scholars congratulate themselves and their colleagues on their sympathetic understanding. Although each of these books has many positive qualities,
as a group they cover too limited a range of the ghetto population. Sometimes these studies even make patently inaccurate
inferences about blacks or unfair generalizations from selective
samples that reinforce, rather than question, the most basic
stereotypes. While the problem is largely one of the ethnographers' collective efforts, it is also sometimes a failure of individual observation.

In American sociology, the image of the black male is particularly one-sided. In the process of developing deeper under-
standings, sociologists casually make demeaning assertions
about the nature of black men. Ulf Hannerz's *Soulside*, for example, is a careful attempt to delineate the relations between
"mainstream" and "ghetto-specific" behavioral patterns and fo-

cuses significantly upon a diverse group of ghetto dwellers to present one of the most heterogeneous portraits of ghetto life. Yet even a sensitive observer like Hannerz uses unsatisfactory evidence to teach generations of his readers about the weak character of black men when he suggests that their autobiographical statements tend to be false. Writing about a janitor not unlike the men at Slim's table, Hannerz tells the following story to illustrate his point about the lack of truthfulness in their stories:

> Mr. Simmons, in his fifties, janitor in an elegant apartment building downtown, told some of his friends about the receptionist in that building:
>
> "You know, today this gal at the front desk said to me, 'You know, Mr. Simmons, I think a gal must be crazy if she don't fall in love with you.' And she's a beauty, brown-skinned, black hair coming down to here (indicating half-way down to the elbow), big legs . . ."
>
> As the conversation was ebbing out a little later, Mr. Simmons suggested that I go with him to see the building. On our way in we passed a middle aged, short haired, not particularly good-looking woman at the reception desk; she answered Mr. Simmons' questions about requests from the residents rather curtly. I had already decided that the girl he had been talking about earlier must work another shift when he said, after we turned around the corner, "Yeah, that's the chick I was telling you about. Ain't she cute?" (P. 110)

Hannerz uses this story to illustrate that some of the autobiographical statements of black men on the corner are "demonstrably untrue." But he is too quick to jump to such a conclusion. Hannerz is making a judgment about beauty that Mr. Simmons simply may not share. It is likely that the black receptionist conducted herself in a formal way in front of Hannerz because he was a white outsider. Had Mr. Simmons been alone in the lobby with the receptionist, her behavior toward him might have been very different. Even if the woman is not precisely the same as Hannerz believed Mr. Simmons described, it is unlikely he would have brought Hannerz to the building immediately after making the statement if he thought Hannerz would reject his assessment of the woman. The evidence Hannerz provides is plausible, but insufficient to suggest by example that black men are prone to tell stories that are "demonstrably untrue." One wonders whether a book making such statements about a white ethnic group would have been so readily accepted by generations of sociologists and their students with as little evidence.

Sociologists, of course, are not the only scholars who make unsupported assertions about the black population. Shelby Steele, the English professor who speaks with such eloquence about innocence and power, is prone to make assertions about the "inertia'" of black people that are overgeneralized from his anecdotes about middle-class blacks. He writes:

> Our ineffectiveness in taking better advantage of our greater opportunity has much to do with this [inertia]. I think there is a specific form of racial anxiety that all blacks are vulnerable to that can, in situations where we must engage in mainstream society, increase our self-doubt and undermine our confidence so that we often back away from the challenges that, if taken, would advance us. I believe this hidden racial anxiety may well now be the strongest barrier to our full participation in the American mainstream; that it is as strong or stronger than the discrimination we face.
>
> . . . We see racism everywhere and miss opportunity even as we stumble over it. . . . The price blacks pay is an ever-escalating poverty that threatens to make the worst off a permanent underclass. (P. 16)

Steele's explanation of the plight of the underclass goes unsupported by any evidence beyond his own observations of middle-class blacks, but it must also be acknowledged that he does not give the impression of being either rigorous or innocent. The back of his book does not advertise that it presents a less stereotyped view of blacks. Indeed, when comparing Steele's assertions with the sociological literature, one notices that sociologists have been prone to offer sweeping impressions of black men which also go beyond their own data. Elijah Anderson writes in *Streetwise*, for example, of his perception of a declining work ethic among young black males. "The young men may have little desire to engage in the 'hard work' their elders performed, even if it were available and had long-term promise" (p. 242). To be sure, I heard such an opinion expressed by some of the men at Slim's table as well, but before the sociologist can make generalizations based upon such assertions, some better data would be necessary. If such a generalization could be supported with evidence beyond the impressions of some of the people with whom Anderson or I spoke, we would have very valuable information. Anderson adds to the impressions of his subjects with this interpretation: "I attribute at least some of this loss of the work ethic indirectly to the social and emotional changes brought on by the civil rights and 'culturally nationalist' movements of the 1960s and 1970s, when so many young blacks, determined to forge a positive new identity, proclaimed that they would never subjugate themselves to whites in the 'slaves'—physically demanding, dirty work—and 'Negro jobs' many of their fathers and grandfathers took for granted" (p. 242).

The ethnographer should always be wary of accepting at face value generalizations made by members of one generation about those of another. This is because it is sometimes possible to find similar statements made during an earlier period with different interpretations put to them. In *Tally's Corner*, for example, a book written almost a quarter century before Anderson's dismissal of today's young black generation, Elliot Liebow discusses the same negative attitude toward manual work among young black males with a completely different interpretation: "That the streetcorner man downgrades manual labor should occasion no surprise. Merton points out that 'the American stigmatization of manual labor . . . *has been found to hold rather uniformly to all social classes*' (emphasis in original; *So-*

cial Theory and Social Structure, p. 145). That he finds no satisfaction in such work should also occasion no surprise: '[There
is] a clear positive correlation between the over-all status of
occupations and the experience of satisfaction in them' (Inkles,
'Industrial Man,' p. 12)."[6] Regardless of his explanation, Liebow's recognition of this phenomenon decades earlier indicates
that Anderson should have been far more wary of making a
generalization about the differences between young black men
today and their own fathers based upon the derogatory observations of his subjects.

It is noteworthy that the personal characteristics of Slim and
his sitting buddies do not conform to those of the black men
described so vividly in sociological accounts of the past quarter
century.[7] One might attempt to dismiss this claim by suggesting
that most ethnographic accounts have simply focused upon
men who belong to the underclass whereas the men at Valois
do not. To be sure, a work like *Tally's Corner,* which shows
black males as lovers, exploiters, and showmen, focuses completely on the lower class and the intermittently employed. But
Hannerz's portrait of Mr. Simmons and Anderson's portrait of
the regulars in *A Place on the Corner* render respectable working black men like those at Valois a distorted personality type—
not to be trusted, or living for material possessions and/or the
constant approval of their associates. As Anderson writes of his
subjects, "in an effort to gain esteem and respect . . . [they]
often resort to exaggerated self-presentations that may include
reports of their vacations, of parties they have attended, of their
jobs, of the upwardly mobile achievements of their relatives,
especially their children, and of the clubs they belong to, of the
fancy restaurants they have visited, and of their good times in
other parts of the city" (p. 67).

Anderson's richly documented account is obviously intended
to represent only one ghetto type, and he makes clear that
many middle- and upper-class whites exhibit these same characteristics, but there is nothing besides the reader's own stereotypes to suggest that this personality is even representative of
the majority of respectable streetcorner men such as Ulf Han-

nerz's Mr. Simmons or the regulars at Slim's table. Yet the tremendous, exclusive popularity of accounts that reinforce images of "niggers in Cadillacs" and "niggers as studs" is illustrative of the unconsciously demeaning image of blacks that emerges from much American sociological work. One is reminded of Ralph Ellison's complaint in 1953 regarding the treatment of blacks in American fiction: What emerges is "an oversimplified clown, a beast, or an angel. Seldom is he drawn as that sensitively focused process of opposites, of good and evil, or instinct and intellect, of passion and spirituality which great literary art has projected as the image of man."[8]

The danger of a literature constituted exclusively of such reports, derived from inaccurate inferences and selective samples, is not only that such images may lead to selective perception.[9] No less dangerous is the manner in which we internalize the images created by ethnographers in a learning process that is geared, not toward the pursuit of truth, but toward the assertion and affirmation of the myth of our own innocence. We come to believe that in carrying around the ethnographer's "enlightened" images we are, on some level, cleansed of prejudice.

Though they go unquestioned, these images should not be accepted at face value simply because their propagators seem to have pure motives. Nor should my own positive portraits of black men establish my own innocence in such a way as to cause my observations to go unquestioned. None of these samples of black men, including my own, can be regarded as typical, but there is no doubt that the sociological views of the black community I have criticized accord mainly with evidence derived from selections based on pre-existing, popular images. The focus is on males who can be found hanging out on street corners and in blues bars, among other places. While the expressive styles described by ethnographers in these spots certainly do exist in the ghetto, there should be a strong presumption against generalizing such findings to the larger black community without compelling evidence. The types of male public gatherings found at Valois serve to suggest, not that

other studies are dead wrong, but that the black male is sufficiently diverse that there are some types within this population
that whites should not only learn about, but can learn from as
well. In this sense, the lapse of ethnography in not capturing
this population has been a failure of the collective enterprise,
rather than the shortcoming of any individual observer.

The collective ethnographic portrait of ghetto-specific masculinity is so one-sided that one would think any positive characteristics men in the ghetto have derive from mainstream
modes of behavior. Because the samples of black men consulted
in these studies have been so limited, generations of students
have been taught that ghetto-specific masculinity is constituted
of, to quote Hannerz, "strong overt concerns with sexual ex-
ploits, toughness and ability to command respect, personal appearance with an emphasis on male clothing fashions, liquor
consumption, and verbal ability" (p. 79). But an open-minded
observer might just as easily entertain the hypothesis that
ghetto-specific masculinity is constituted of extraordinary "caring behavior" as characterized by the substitute kinship tie illustrated by the relationship of Slim and Bart, as well as resolve, pride, and sincerity, as embodied in the other stories of
the men at Valois. We would need more information, both
about other black groups and the wider society, before we could
draw such a conclusion. But these data alone give us reason to
suspect that the existing definition of ghetto-specific masculinity is far too narrowly focused.

Part of the problem with these portraits lies in the theoretical framework which informs them. Since the 1920s, American
sociologists—and especially the ethnographers among them—
have been influenced by a view of human nature which largely
derives from the philosophy of George Herbert Mead, especially as it was interpreted by Herbert Blumer, and as it found
its fulfillment in the work of Howard S. Becker and Erving
Goffman.[10] This approach to the study of man—symbolic interactionism—views the self as created through the process of interaction itself and sees man as engaged in constant mechanisms of adjustment as he decides who he is based upon what

others think of him. Although I have much sympathy for this approach, especially as it is represented in Becker's work, it has probably been taken too far in much contemporary sociology, thereby resulting in a one-dimensional, underautonomized image of man. When fieldworkers enter settings convinced of the universal applicability of such perspectives, they are in constant danger of failing to allow for the possibility of an autonomous human being; they risk not perceiving a core self when it exists. [11]

The problem is that black men can be found in a wide range of places, but the only public contexts from which sociological images of black men are derived are places where expressive styles would be most expected to manifest themselves and where sociologists see good opportunities to apply their theories of symbolic interactionism. Thus, on a street corner where a heterogeneous group of winos, hoodlums, and mainstreamers gather, there is greater reason to expect personalities to be constantly engaged in battles over definitions of situations. The different identities are more likely to be in a state of flux where various social types are negotiating and adjusting their self-conceptions and attempting to define others. Even at Valois, the men seem to be most defensive when they feel challenged by different categories of persons. On those rare occasions when conflicts occur between black regulars and students, for example, we can see the same processes at work. Depending on the situation, the same men may demonstrate elements of various interaction styles.

Some sociologists will be disposed to defend their portraits by arguing that "those who represent traditional liberal views on social issues have been [too] reluctant to discuss openly or, in some instances, even to acknowledge the sharp increase in social pathologies in ghetto communities." [12] I do not believe sociologists should hide or suppress any truths. My qualms about the ethnographic tradition of writing about blacks is not its effort to speak openly about the ghettos; to the contrary, sociology cannot survive the burdens of political correctness. There are no benefits to be accrued by an inaccurate and sanitized portrait. The goal should always be accurate description. Indeed, this is why I have emphasized in these pages that, despite their own desire to be understood by others, the black regulars at Valois are no less prone to indulge inaccurate stereotypes of other groups. The works discussed here constitute the dominant tradition of sociological writing about blacks. Because these books are written by scholars with liberal credentials or because they claim to render a less stereotyped portrait (the two most common ways of establishing innocence) and because on some level each of these books has made some progress in liberating blacks from the images that are used to oppress them, when they confirm blacks in other stereotypes with insubstantial evidence they are even more insidious in their influence than an explicitly racist account, which would have no prospect of acceptance. This is evident in the wide respect the whole body of ethnography on black men has achieved, despite its tendency to make generalizations that would be intolerable if made about white ethnic groups without strong evidence or if made by anyone with a strong political agenda. When innocence, rather than truth, becomes the license for our assertions, we can get away with saying many things that are not supported by evidence.

The best proof for this proposition lies in an examination of the praise garnered by a popular journalistic account, Nicholas Lemann's *The Promised Land: The Great Black Migration and How It Changed America*. The book is largely an account of southern sharecroppers who moved to the North, ultimately to live in housing projects on Chicago's South Side. It is also a study of how policymakers in Washington and Chicago responded to ghetto poverty. Lemann leaves the impression that the migration changed America by transplanting a culture beset by pathological poverty to northern cities. The author focuses on former sharecroppers in order to write about the nation's response to poverty, implying that they typify the northern black underclass. Both ideas, which are clearly false, provide a misleading interpretation of one of the great events in African American history. Yet, they were accepted uncritically by reviewers. I believe the book's reception cannot be separated from the manner in which its author established his own innocence as an entitlement to make generalizations about the black migration that were particularly inaccurate and unflattering.

This is best illustrated by comparing *The Promised Land* with earlier articles the author wrote about the migration. When his theory was first published in the *Atlantic* in 1986, Lemann argued that "every aspect of the underclass culture in the ghettos is directly traceable to roots of the South." He said that this "distinctive culture is now the greatest barrier to progress by the black underclass." Elaborating the implications of these conservative views for public policy, he wrote:

> The new immigrants of the ghettos (Koreans, Vietnamese, West Indians) have in many cases settled in the ghettos, and so should have experienced all of the reverse incentives, but they have quickly become successful, because they maintain a separate culture. The negative power of the ghetto culture all but guarantees that any attempt to solve the problems of the underclass in the ghettos won't work—the culture is too strong by now. Any solution that does work, whatever it does about welfare and unemployment, will also have to get people physically away from the ghettos.[13]

Lemann's views earned him praise from many conservatives, but he was roundly attacked by prominent liberals including William Julius Wilson, who devoted part of his book, *The Truly Disadvantaged,* to discrediting Lemann's black migration thesis. Wilson wrote in 1987 that "systematic research . . . consistently shows Southern-born blacks who have migrated to the urban North experience greater economic success in terms of employment rates, earnings and welfare dependency than do those urban blacks who were born in the North" (p. 55).

When Lemann published his 1991 book, he did an aboutface on the issue of the potential of government:

In the specific case of the ghettos, the idea that the government can't accomplish anything is a smokescreen obscuring the useful and encouraging results of a quarter century's worth of research on antipoverty programs—research of a kind that didn't exist when the war on poverty began.

Programs that come under the banner of "intervention," in which the government becomes a guiding presence in the lives of the ghetto poor, do demonstrably work.[14]

In the nexus between innocence and power, Lemann's embrace of big government in the book established his liberal credentials. Whereas a prominent scholar on the left like Wilson had previously attacked Lemann's articles, when essentially the same theory was published in book form, eminent liberal reviewers took for granted many of the very same assertions which unfairly demeaned the significance of the great black migration, and which Wilson had previously demolished. (In a defense of the subsequent book, Lemann even claimed that Wilson had read *The Promised Land* in manuscript without raising any objections.) Virtually none of the reviews pointed out that Lemann's book was wrong in implying that the underclass migrants he depicts are typical of the blacks who went north. The reviews did not take Lemann to task for failing to center his analysis on the majority of migrants who helped establish the black middle class, working class, and lower working class in northern cities.[15]

Lemann's new credentials gave him a license that might not have been granted to one who stuck to his earlier conservative claims about the power and role of government in the original *Atlantic* articles. In *The Promised Land*, setting the tone for all that follows, he writes, "Black sharecropper society on the eve of the introduction of the mechanical cotton picker was the equivalent of big-city ghetto society in many ways. It was the national center of illegitimate child bearing and of the female-headed family" (p. 31). He gives the impression that there is a link between the migration—the subject of his book—and the emergence of pathology in the northern ghettos. He does not inform the reader that contemporary evidence demonstrates that sharecroppers were not representative of the majority of migrants. The typical migrant was more successful than the Northern-born black. Nor does he inform his reader that, as David Whitman has pointed out in "The Great Sharecropper Success Story," "Black women in the rural South were more likely to be married than were urban black women living in the South or North from at least 1910 to 1960" (p. 14).

Yet even more than the implications of Lemann's words themselves, the structure of his book demonstrates the length to which the media sometimes go to emphasize disproportionately the existence of the underclass. He places studies from 1932 and earlier supporting his theme at the front, while dismissing decades of the most contemporary counterevidence in one small paragraph at the back of the book. Thus, Lemann refers in his opening chapter to the eminent pre–World War II sociologist, E. Franklin Frazier, who thought that lower-class blacks' social pathologies in the North replicated southern patterns. Lemann devotes only two scant paragraphs to the overwhelming contemporary evidence that contradicts his thesis (p. 287). No wonder so many reviewers believed Lemann presented the definitive account of America's urban problems. Had the overwhelming data disclosing the migrants' relative success been made as prominent as Lemann's call for a new $10–25 billion antipoverty initiative (his concluding chapter was largely devoted to making assertions about the potential of government to help these problems), unknowing reviewers would have immediately understood that the main topics he covers—the War on Poverty and the underclass—are incidental to an assessment of "the great black migration and how it changed America."

Lemann ultimately justified his decision to make Ruby Haynes, a former Mississippi sharecropper who later lived in Chicago's housing projects, the book's main character by stating that she was typical of the sharecropper society she grew up in.[16] But this is irrelevant since the objective of *The Promised Land*—and the grounds upon which it garnered praise—was its pretense of assessing the significance of the black migration in shaping American society. Sharecroppers were simply not typical of the migration. They had lower earnings than the larger migrant population which, on the whole, did better than northern-born blacks. Since Ruby Haynes is not typical of the migration, it doesn't matter that she might be typical of the sharecroppers.

A discussion of the Lemann book serves to indict the most influential institutions of the mass media in their tendency to make the most "respectable" patterns in black life invisible. *The Promised Land*, excerpted in the *Los Angeles Times*, the *Atlantic*, and the *New York Times Magazine* (with the title "Four Generations in the Projects"), received widespread acclaim that it did not merit and focused undue attention on the pathological underclass, especially for a work about the migration that should have included more about black respectability.

The widespread attention the book received was due to the fact that many reviewers who are normally expert at asserting their own greater sensitivity to demeaning and inaccurate stereotypes were so influenced by Lemann's liberal credentials that, when he confirmed inaccurate stereotypes of blacks, they saw no need to check even widely available statistics before joining in a chorus of praise. There is no doubt that the thesis even seems plausible to those who do not embrace Lemann's liberal agenda, because in focusing on the atypical, least successful migrants, it confirms the dominant, stereotypical image of blacks. Typical of the righteous tone which accompanied many of the reviews was a *New York Times* editorial which asserted that paper's own moral superiority by suggesting that *The Promised Land* has the power to "educate" the American public, which it accused of settling for racial stereotypes based on "profound ignorance." In light of the available data, Lemann's champions in the media were no less guilty than the population they disdain.

The antics of blacks in the works of sociologists and journalists are studied as the functional equivalent of anthropology's great subject, primitive or savage man. The aspiration to respectability within the black population is largely ignored or misrepresented. Indeed, the discipline of sociology got off to a wrong start in this regard as early as World War II, with the epigraph to the first great ethnography of the black community, *Black Metropolis*. St. Clair Drake and Horace Cayton could not have known how selective would be the implication of the quotation by Robert E. Park which began their book, indicating that the motives of urban life and culture are the same as those of primitive people. Park emphasized that the motives of the latter are more subtle and complicated. But there is a dimension to all of this work which suggests that the progressive discipline of sociology, and many journalists as well, still portray black people as though they are primitive.

CHAPTER

10

Conclusion

The black regulars at Valois sense that they are isolated from institutions which serve to propagate and maintain symbols of decency that were once embodied in ghetto life but now also seem to have declined in mainstream culture. They feel separate from human beings like themselves who strongly desire to participate in modes of conduct that testify to respectability.

The fact that a powerful combination of scholars and journalists has abdicated its responsibility to look beyond folk images in understanding ghetto life has relegated a very large number of blacks (who might otherwise be empowered) into oblivion and has emboldened other blacks—a few of whom are sincere, but many more of whom are demagogues and hustlers—to capture the spotlight and become spokesmen for those who are the media's focus. Knowing they alone are taken to represent the black community, these emboldened blacks state their world view with complete self-confidence while others who have their doubts retreat into silence. The media's emphasis on these figures plays into the hands of those who would conflate traditional civil rights leaders with black extremist politicians.[1] Those whose views accord with the standard of respectability but who are more confused and less thick-skinned than Slim and his sitting buddies may be deterred from publicly asking reflective moral questions about the pathologies that threaten their lives every day. Such behavior is consistent with social scientific evidence that suggests that human beings, perceiving that those who share their views have become weaker, grow less confident in expressing opinions, or even fall silent. As the German sociologist Elisabeth Noelle-Neumann wrote in a study of public opinion, "one side in a controversy will be active and open in its 'talk' while the other side, though not necessarily smaller in numbers, perhaps even larger, holds its peace."[2]

The morally isolated live with a strong sense that the very definition of blackness in America presented by the extremists has come to preclude them. They resent those whose prominence in the media has led them to believe they can monopolize the very definition of blackness itself. In *Soulside,* Ulf Hannerz recognized that many blacks are ambivalent about living in accordance with mainstream values because doing so demands a certain disavowal of their black identity.[3] But this is especially true when the definition of blackness is monopolized by those who would idealize it in a false dichotomy between primordial identity and the standard of respectability and who would explain conditions in the ghetto by focusing completely upon how society blames the victim to the exclusion of discussions about personal responsibility.

The world view of individuals like the black regulars at Valois is constituted of no fewer contradictions than that of the dominant white majority. This is because, like most Americans, they feel confusion about slum conditions, a certain lack of confidence in their ability to withstand them, and fear. But they have no less conviction that many of those who would claim to represent or portray their interests—including journalists and extremist black leaders—must be called to account for their reports, rhetoric, and action. The paucity of visible leadership and public symbols embodying and crystallizing the moral components of a separate, authentic black image symbolized by a belief in personal responsibility, integration, and the importance of social order with which they can identify helps explain the tremendous desire on the part of such people for informal, private primary groups of the kind they form at Valois.

Collective life at the cafeteria helps black regulars overcome the aloneness created by their sense of living in a moral vacuum. In contemplating the collective life formed by Slim and his sitting buddies, then, one has an opportunity to understand better what it means for human beings to experience actual membership in their society. Unlike most Americans, many ghetto dwellers cannot—by virtue of the power they exercise, the material objects they possess, or the institutions to which they belong—take for granted their membership in the larger society.

In asking what it is about mainstream society that makes it the focus for some ghetto dwellers, one risks being misunderstood. To begin, such a question might be taken to imply that blacks are somehow deficient because they are not completely part of white society, while whites lose nothing by not participating in black society. Such an interpretation would miss a central point of this endeavor. In the stories of Slim and Bart, one of the white men, Hughes, saw himself living up to standards that were embodied in the black man, Slim. White men can learn much about the possibilities of the masculine role from black men who have had to engage in adaptations unusual in white society.

In coming to a cafeteria in the integrated Hyde Park district, some of these men are expressing a desire to participate in the larger, more comprehensive society with which most other Americans can more easily assume a connection. Although the black regulars find contact with white society fulfilling, one should not infer that what they discover in the wider white society is in any way superior because it is white. The wider society, rather than simply being a civilizing influence for these men, is a vehicle for them to express their own civility. Their passage from the ghetto to the wider society does not entail the abdication of a former culture. The black regulars are, to be sure, not culturally self-subsistent, but within the larger society they have formed a collectivity with many of the characteristics of their former community, the old ghetto described decades ago in Drake and Cayton's *Black Metropolis*.

The partial, daily incorporation into mainstream society does not represent a simple adoption of values that are white or somehow not their own. The greater order that is embodied in cafeteria life was once a characteristic of ghetto life as well and, despite some stereotypes, still exists in some parts of the ghetto. Participation in the wider society ultimately confers on the regulars the respectability of their own cultural traditions.

This book was inspired by a pioneering tradition of urban sociology that seeks to examine those ways in which city life promotes conflict between groups that respond to one another as categories, while promoting solidarity between those who share a consciousness of kind.[4] This is a perspective that emphasizes competition and social contrast as the most essential constituents of city life. We have seen that the black regulars sometimes differentiate themselves from other categories with whom they share space. At the same time, however, it has been necessary to diverge from that tradition at certain points. For at the cafeteria the highest form of respectability resulted not from contrasts between one's group and others in the setting, but from positive relations with other categories of persons. To understand the nature of respectability among human beings in low-income neighborhoods, it has been necessary to describe the need they feel to enter into a relationship with their society. This disposition implies the existence and significance of relations with human beings who are different from oneself. The image of self in such a context is the product of a process more subtle and complex than that described by the phrase "compare and contrast."

As long as violence and the decline of social order remain the most salient symbols of ghetto life for inhabitants of these districts, primary groups emblematic of morality are likely to continue to exist. Perhaps it is in the nature of isolated individuals with beliefs and values essential to the respectability of a people to form collectivities with other like-minded people. Nor will this group or assemblies of its kind die out when its present older members die. Such persons will be replenished by a younger generation who will likely live with even more cynicism than their predecessors, but also with a basic desire for social order. Whether they will be as stable and autonomous as Valois's regulars is unlikely, given America's worsening position in the world economy. But even this, hardly a closed question, will depend upon economic and cultural developments of the coming decades.

The changes that have occurred in these neighborhoods are not merely a reflection of the stereotyping of blacks perpetuated by journalists and sociologists. Nor will these changes be erased or corrected with simple solutions such as providing better jobs or presenting nicer, sanitized images, which are necessary but insufficient conditions for change. The decline in the ghetto of the values of restraint, family life, and social responsibility reflects cultural changes in the wider society which must transform itself before it can expect the values of the ghettos to change. Better jobs and nicer images just may not be enough at this point to make men like the regulars feel that they can control their neighborhoods, that they can act together to impose social control, and that they can hold themselves up as models to be admired.

Certainly, without a consciousness of their own significance, the "respectable" black masses cannot be harnessed to serve as an active force in maintaining stability within their own communities. One might even go so far as to say that the wider society must be challenged to change its own distorted values before conventional ghetto blacks like Slim can expect to be taken seriously by those members of the black population who aren't listening to them now.[5] As they stand, the messages of the wider society reinforce all of the values men like these observe destroying their neighborhoods, making the stands they take all the more lonely. Certainly the Democratic Party has done little to stand up to this decline. At the same time, the media give undue attention to the extremist black leaders who monopolize the definition of blackness and thereby silence contradiction. Yet, despite many of their conservative social values, these men are not like the "disenfranchised" white liberals who moved to the Republican column during the 1980s. Because of their deeply felt antagonism to symbols of the right wing, these men do not look to the Republican Party without coming up empty-handed. Who will speak for them?

There is a sense in America today that it is not only the black male who is in trouble, that the very conception of middle-class white manhood offered by movies, literature, social science, and the news media is also somehow wanting. The emergence of a new men's movement in the 1990s heralded by Robert Bly's bestselling *Iron John: A Book about Men* is a reaction to what many men regard as the empty and incomplete images provided by clichés and rhetoric of the 1960s and 1970s.[6] As Bly says,

> Historically, the male has changed considerably in the past thirty years. Back then there was a person we could call the '50's male, who was hardworking, responsible, fairly well disciplined. . . . If you were a man you were supposed to like football games, be aggressive, stick up for the United States, never cry, and always provide. But this image of the male lacked feminine space. It lacked some sense of flow, it lacked compassion. . . . Then during the '60's, another sort of male appeared. . . . As men began to look at women and at their concerns, some men began to see their own feminine side and pay attention to it. . . . Now there's something wonderful about all this— the step of the male bringing forth his own feminine consciousness is an important one—and yet I have the sense there is something wrong. The male in the past twenty years has become more thoughtful, more gentle. But by this process he has not become more free. He's a nice boy who now not only pleases his mother but also the young

woman he is living with. I see the phenomenon of what I would call the "soft male" all over the country today. . . . Many of these men are unhappy. There's not much energy in them. They are life-preserving but not exactly life-giving.[7]

Bly argues that contemporary men have lost touch with the deep masculine side of their psyches because fathers are less prominent in the lives of their sons and women are incapable of initiating young men into society. Fathers more typically establish visitation rights on weekends or spend long hours at the office. Although Bly does not say when the latter was not true of successful professional and managerial men, he and his followers firmly believe that fathers, uncles, grandfathers, and male neighbors have abdicated their responsibilities as mentors. Bly reflects on male initiation rituals in many parts of the world to point out the importance of mentoring.

The men's movement's ideas are often dismissed as pop psychology, and indeed they are difficult to verify empirically, but they are having a great impact upon the way many men think about their lives. One cultural experience that might enhance these reflections is that of the American black population, and especially that of the older ghettos in which men like the regulars at Valois were "reared up." Many of these men grew up in homes where the father was at least as absent as in today's white middle-class families. Yet, these are still people whom the contemporary men's movement would envy. They are consistently inner-directed and firm, and they act with resolve; their images of self-worth are not derived from material possessions or the approval of others; they are disciplined ascetics with respect for wisdom and experience; usually humble, they can be quiet, sincere, and discreet, and they look for those qualities in their friends. They are sensitive, but not "soft" in any sense that the men's movement sees as the basis of its gender crisis. They know how to put their foot down, and how to "show their swords."[8]

These are human beings who, in treating and associating with whites, seek to live by the standards of a civil society and who live with appreciation for the kind of primordial community in which they were "reared up." The black regulars gain standing with one another through their sincerity. A man is more likely to earn respect through his honesty about some failing than by legitimating some bold claim. One does not become "somebody" in the cafeteria by making assertions that are then accepted or "blown away" by the crowd. Rather, genuineness and honesty are the characteristics that are most admired. When men speak of why they care so much for Slim, they say that he tells them "what he thinks." Whereas some men will cover up what's happened to them, he will "come around and say it like it is." They do not demonstrate a need to compensate for their failures through an exaggeration of their personal qualities. The black regulars have found a place where they can be themselves without competing for the regard or positive evaluation of others.

Black men like the regulars are responsive, sensitive, and receptive, but not "soft." Indeed, the inability to be fierce that Bly sees in the relationships of today's "soft" man is simply not characteristic of black men like these. They learn that when it is time to take a risk or when resolve is needed, they cannot afford to "come up short." As the men's movement searches for a masculinity it can admire, it might begin by studying black males of this sort and attempting to comprehend how the older ghettos formed men of such character. Indeed, sociologists and psychologists need to explore with greater care the hypothesis that the adaptations of some black men have produced at least some variants of a ghetto-specific masculinity with positive characteristics that might serve as a model to men in the wider society.

Not long after Ovie Carter, who is himself a black male, began shooting photographs for this book, he gave me a stack of pictures including the one that appears at the front of this chapter. I put them on a table in my apartment.

One afternoon a friend came to visit me and picked up the photos while we talked.

"Are these pictures of the men you wrote about?" he queried.

"Yes."

"Do they have homes? Or . . ."

Before he could continue, I told him that none of the men in the pictures were homeless and that they all had jobs. He seemed embarrassed. I felt bad. I thought it would make him feel better if he knew that most people asked similar questions. I recounted the two most common things I was asked when I told friends I was writing about black men: "Is it safe?" and "Do you live on the streets with them?"

I hoped that this would make him feel better, but I had miscalculated. I had made him feel that he was part of a category to which he did not feel he properly belonged. And even worse, I had spoken about that category as if I were somehow more innocent than all of its members.

Only a few months before, when Ovie Carter and I had spent the summer working together, I created a situation that demonstrated my own insensitivity. We had gone to a local used book store to take a photograph of some of the major ethnographic works by American sociologists gathered together on a wooden shelf. I had carried with me copies of most of the books we would use. The idea was to go to the black studies section in the back of the store, place the volumes on a shelf, and photograph them.

As we entered, Ovie asked me if I thought we needed permission to take pictures. The store was rather busy, and I knew we would be shooting in the back where few store personnel pass by. Most important, I had spent so much time in the store that I thought its personnel knew me.

"What do you think?" I asked.

"It might not be a bad idea."

As we contemplated the issue, the only store personnel I saw were ringing up a long line at the cash register. It didn't seem worth it to me to stand around waiting to get someone's attention. Ovie agreed to go ahead with our original plan.

In the back of the store, I removed the books from my bag and placed them on the shelf. Ovie began shooting.

Suddenly the store's manager came up behind us. He volunteered that what we were doing was okay, but that he would have appreciated it if we had let him know.

As Ovie completed his work, I began taking the books off the shelf. I realized that the manager, who was still present, had no way of knowing that the books belonged to me, so I gave a fuller explanation. He was very understanding.

As we rode away from the store in Ovie's car, he noted the difference in the way we were disposed to handle the situation. In a very sensitive way, he pointed out something I knew in theory but had not acted on in the situation: As a white man I go through life believing I can take liberties that black men would never think of taking. One can only imagine what would have happened if a black man had been seen putting books in a bag. This is why Ovie had suggested that we ask permission to engage in an act that I conceived as harmless. Despite his sensitivity, I felt stupid. If anyone should have been aware of the situation, it was a sociologist who was writing about black men.

Given my experience with Ovie, I was the last person to allow my friend to feel deflated about his comments on the photograph a few months later. But the fact is that we live at a time when interactions like this one are so commonplace that we engage in them without reflection. Many people use their own supposed innocence to inflate themselves or allow others to feel deflated. Shelby Steele's words deserve repeating: "Once inflated we are entitled; we are in fact licensed to go after the power our innocence tells us we deserve." Recognizing this, when we note that the men at Slim's table are tarnished unfairly with reputations as destroyers, as lovers and exploiters, as "wine heads" and drug addicts, and as the seekers of constant approval and affirmation from their fellow men, the purpose must not be to attain an attribution of innocence for them or ourselves, but truth. Truth is not the same as innocence because truth is a vehicle for solving problems whereas innocence merely seeks power.

In chapter 2, I noted that the men at Slim's table feel short-changed by movies and magazines which give the impression that black men make only tentative commitments to their jobs, romanticize shallow relationships, live without self-esteem, and position themselves to catch the attention of fellow loungers with acts of exaggerated self-presentation. But we cannot ignore the fact that those same men are not above overgeneralizing about middle-class blacks, white university students, and lower-class blacks. Nor can it be said that these men don't monitor others for innocence. One need only recall the discussions about the university's police force, its campus buses, its crime maps, and the incident in which a student offended the men when he seemed surprised that some didn't have children, to recognize that, like other Americans, these men will sometimes increase their own power in a situation by reminding others of their guilt. What emphasizes the extent to which these situations are indeed power plays is that one senses that, unlike many Americans, the men at Slim's table are beyond believing in the possibility of racial innocence. This does not mean that there are not differing levels of guilt, as when a man inquires whether his companion at the table is a "die-hard conservative." But in most of their interaction they simply do not concern themselves with demonstrating such innocence to others. They see their communities coming apart and believe that more important battles must also be waged at this time. They speak candidly about conditions in the ghetto and the wider society. This makes them different from many politicians, journalists, professors, and middle-class blacks and whites who place a higher premium on portraying their own "essential goodness in relation to others" than in searching for truth.

"Do they have homes?" Would the individual who asked have felt any better if he had known about my own lack of sensitivity in the bookstore? Probably not. Like many Americans, he holds himself up to such high standards that it would have been irrelevant to him. Like many Americans, he wishes to think of himself as a "good" person. But I had no right to let that conversation end with the impression that I was somehow less guilty than he was. When we stop trying to feel good about ourselves, or to increase our own power by asserting our innocence, we can begin to look for answers by searching for truth.

Acknowledgments

This book and the fieldwork it is based on emerged directly from Professor Edward Shils's seminars in sociological theory held in Harper 155 at the University of Chicago. As the university celebrates its centennial, Professor Shils, himself teaching full-time in his own ninth decade, is its model professor, a monument of generosity and learning, elegantly deployed. I wish to express my gratitude to him for his extraordinary kindness and insight over many years.

I also wish to thank Professor Howard S. Becker, who taught me the field methods of the Chicago school. His encouragement during lonely years in the field mattered a great deal. I am grateful for his wise guidance on this project.

As an urban ethnographer one could have no greater example than Professor Gerald D. Suttles. I benefited enormously from his advice and counsel, as well as our disagreements about the urban ethnographic tradition.

Mr. Ovie Carter, who shot the pictures for this book, is a photographer of extraordinary sensitivity. For his friendship and collaboration on this project, I express my deep gratitude. It has been a special pleasure to work with him.

For their wise substantive and editorial comments on an earlier version I wish to thank Professors Bob Blauner, Christopher Jencks, and Peggy Davis. At a number of earlier stages, I also benefited from the kindness of Morris Janowitz, Joseph Ben-David, Roger Michener, William A. Sampson, Gary King, Leonard S. Davenport, Robert Fleischaker, John A. Beyrer, Billie Crawford, Christine Schnusenburg, Stephen Presser, Michael Rea, Peter Kretzmer, and Henry Finn, M.D.

Kerwin Duneier, Candi Duneier, Muriel and Arthur King, Fred and Shelly Duneier, Phil Fruman, Jeffery C. Cohen, Monica Feinberg, Louis Petrich, Paul Zarowin, Russell and Katie Adler, Melissa Bomes, Regina Titunik-Yoshikawa, Kavitha Rao, Gail Letzter, David Weiner, Michael Higginbotham, Ronald Gunville, Joshua Karsh, Lois David, Susan Muhlhauser, and David Waldman were particularly helpful. Jonathan A. Segal's friendship (and his generosity with an excellent personal collection of works of the Chicago school of sociology) was very important.

After the fieldwork and a few rough drafts of most of the chapters were completed, I packed the materials and left Chicago to attend the New York University School of Law. During my first and second years as a law student, the current version—which seems to bear almost no relation to the original—was written. The N.Y.U. School of Law is an exciting intellectual environment, uniquely supportive of students, with many distractions in the form of course offerings, speakers, and lively exchanges among an extraordinary collection of pupils and devoted professors. It provided a perfect environment in which to complete the book. I wish to thank Professor James B. Jacobs for his support and encouragement during this period. I would also wish to acknowledge the collegiality of all of my fellow students at N.Y.U., and in particular Josh Goldfein, Joseph Saunders, Carl Thomas, Yodon Thonden, Jennifer Wolfe, and Adam Winkler.

Doug Mitchell, senior editor of the University of Chicago Press, gave superb editorial advice that helped me grow as an ethnographer. Wilma Ebbitt made a number of extremely helpful suggestions. Most importantly, I express my gratitude to Penelope Gunville for her intellectual support and love. She lived this project with me, believed in it before anybody else, and guided it from the beginning.

The most difficult part of writing this book was going away. I thank the proprietors and regulars at Valois Cafeteria. They are always in my heart.

Notes

Chapter 1

1. For an excellent article, see Mary Jo Bane and David Ellwood, "Is American Business Working for the Poor?" *Harvard Business Review*, September–October, 1991, pp. 58–66. See also Ellwood, *Poor Support: Poverty and the American Family* (New York: Basic Books, 1988).

2. In this book, I adopt the assumptions about social class enunciated by Christopher Jencks, who writes,

We use terms such as "middle class" and "underclass" because we know that occupation, income, educational credentials, cognitive skills, a criminal record, out-of-wedlock childbearing, and other personal characteristics are somewhat correlated with one another. Class labels provide a shorthand device for describing people who differ along many of these dimensions simultaneously. The term "middle class," for example, evokes someone who has attended college, holds a steady job, earns an adequate income, got married before having children, and has never murdered, raped, robbed, or assaulted anyone. The term "underclass," in contrast, conjures up a chronically jobless high school dropout who has had two or three children out of wedlock, has very little money to support them, and probably has either a criminal record or a history of welfare dependence.

Relatively few people fit either of these stereotypes perfectly. Many people are "middle class" in some respects, "working class" in others, and "underclass" in still others. Those who use class labels always assume, however, that everyone is a member of some class or another. In order to assign everyone to a class, they allow their classes to be internally heterogeneous. If they assign people to classes on the basis of how they make their living, for example, they allow the members of these classes to differ with regard to income, educational credentials, cognitive skills, family structure, and arrest record. Everyone who stops to think recognizes that the world is untidy in this sense. We use class labels precisely because we want to make the world seem tidier than it is. The purpose of these labels is to draw attention to the differences between classes. But by emphasizing differences between classes, such labels inevitably encourage us to forget about the much larger differences that exist *within* classes.

See Christopher Jencks, *Rethinking Social Policy* (Cambridge, Mass.: Harvard University Press, 1992).

Thus a man like Ted, who works for *Playboy* magazine in the photographic lab and retired from a long career in the army, might be considered a member of the working class by virtue of the jobs he has held. His use of large words might demonstrate a verbal ability associated with a middle-class education. His many trips abroad might also show a middle-class orientation, and his views may fluctuate between a working-class orientation most of the time and a middle-class orientation on occasions.

A man like Jackson, a crane operator and longshoreman, who saw much of the world during the Korean war, will engage in a conversation about Paris that might normally be expected from a middle-class person. He reads newspapers and a high school history book and has a working knowledge of western history. But he lives in a small one-bedroom apartment, has no telephone, and writes all of his checks at the currency exchange. His wages put him below the poverty line. He has a small wardrobe and very few possessions and can only afford to eat one meal a day.

Because of the difficulties involved in any system of classification, I am wary of making claims regarding what these men typify within the class structure of the black community. Though most of their occupations, lifestyles, and values place them in the working and lower-working class, I leave it to readers to draw their own conclusions for individual members of the group. With regard to the composition of the black class structure, William Julius Wilson writes, "To be somewhat schematic, of the 29 million American blacks, about 20 percent are in the professional middle class, with another 15 percent in noncredentialed white-collar positions. About 33 percent are working class, with half of them vulnerable to job loss, and 33 percent poor. I'd say about half of that poor population is truly disadvantaged, a sort of destitute population." "The Poor Image of Black Men," *New Perspectives Quarterly* 8, no. 3 (summer 1991): 26.

Readers can draw their own conclusions from the table (cited in Martin Kilson and Clement Cottingham, "Thinking about Race Relations," *Dissent*, Fall 1991, p. 521), which summarizes some relevant statistics.

3. "The margins of the ghetto can be scenes of tension as they become gentrified and are slowly absorbed by a wider community made up primarily of middle- and upper-income people who for the most part are white." See Elijah Anderson, *Streetwise: Race, Class, and Change in an Urban Community* (Chicago: University of Chicago Press, 1990), p. 1.

4. Variations of such relations have been referred to as pseudo-kinship ties. See Elliot Liebow, *Tally's Corner: A Study of Negro Streetcorner Men* (Boston: Little, Brown, 1967), pp. 166–67. "One of the most striking aspects of these overlapping relationships is the use of kinship as a model for the friend relationship. . . . The most common form of the pseudo-kin relationship between two men is known as 'going for brothers.' This means, simply, that two men agree to present themselves as brothers to the outside world and to deal with one another on the same basis." For similar observations, see Elijah Anderson, *A Place on the Corner* (Chicago: University of Chicago Press, 1978), pp. 17–23. Because there was no effort on the part of my subjects to present themselves as kin or pass these relationships off as genuine, I have refrained from using the word "pseudo" in describing their relations. The substitute kinship tie is characterized by the assumption of obligations normally associated with kinship. For the best discussions of kin-structured social networks, see Carol Stack, *All Our Kin: Strategies of Survival in a Black Community* (New York: Harper Colophon Books, 1974) and Ward Goodenough, *Description and Comparison in Cultural Anthropology* (Chicago: Aldine Publishing Co., 1970).

5. Hughes told me about this conversation after it occurred. I often

asked him questions about conversations and occurrences between him and Bart or between him and Slim. When it was not awkward, I often verified Hughes's version with either Slim or Bart. Once I asked Hughes about a particular conversation years after it occurred, because I thought I had lost my notes on it. Hughes told me what he recalled of the conversation. Weeks later I found the old notes and discovered that Slim had used precisely the same words to describe the conversation a few years before. I only used reports which I felt certain had a high degree of reliability. The occasions on which I asked various subjects what others had said were normal conversations and occurred through normal interaction rather than formal interviews. Unless otherwise indicated, this is the only chapter in which I quote from a conversation at which I was not present. Most of the notes I took for more than four years with the men at Valois were written down afterward, upon my return home.

6. For a more complete discussion of stereotypes of black men in American sociology, see chapter 9.

7. See Richard Majors, "Cool Pose: The Proud Signature of Black Survival," in Michael S. Kimmel and Michael A. Messner, *Men's Lives* (New York: Macmillan Publishing Co., 1989), pp. 83–87.

8. Morris Janowitz, Introduction to *W. I. Thomas on Social Organization and Social Personality* (Chicago: University of Chicago Press, 1966).

Chapter 2

1. "Study Shows Racial Imbalance in Penal System," *New York Times*, February 27, 1990, p. 18.

2. "'One in 4 Young Black Men Is in Custody,' a Study Says," *New York Times*, October 4, 1990, p. 6.

3. This data is reported in "Voices of the Endangered American Black Male," *Boston Globe*, September 4, 1991, Living Section, p. 53.

4. Everett Hughes, *The Sociological Eye* (New Brunswick, N.J.: Transaction Books, 1984), p. 311.

5. See S. Wyatt and J. A. Fraser, *The Effects of Monotony in Work* (London: His Majesty's Stationery Office, 1929), Elton Mayo, *The Human Problems of an Industrial Civilization* (New York: Macmillan Co., 1933).

6. These personality characteristics are similar to those described in Wyatt and Fraser, *The Effects of Monotony.*

7. Many accounts of African American language patterns take note of insults which tend to be ritualized. The insults at Valois do not take the form of rhymes or other stereotyped language. For comparisons with ritual insults, see William Labov, "Rules for Ritual Insults," in David Sudnow, ed., *Studies in Social Interaction* (New York: Free Press, 1978); see also Gerald D. Suttles, "Friendship as a Social Institution," in George J. McCall et al., *Social Relationships* (Chicago: Aldine Publishing Co., 1970), pp. 95–135. For a comparison, see Anderson, *A Place on the Corner.*

8. Liebow, *Tally's Corner,* pp. 137–43.

9. This was the phrase used by Elijah Anderson to describe the behavioral tendencies of lower- and working-class men on the street-corner. See Anderson, *A Place on the Corner,* p. 51.

Chapter 3

1. St. Clair Drake and Horace Cayton, *Black Metropolis* (New York: Harcourt, Brace, & Co., 1945), p. 12.

2. Nicholas Lemann, *The Promised Land* (New York: Alfred A. Knopf, 1991), p. 64.

3. This point is made by David Whitman in a comprehensive and insightful discussion of the great black migration: "The Great Share-cropper Success Story," *Public Interest* 104 (Summer 1991): 3.

4. E. Franklin Frazier, *The Negro Family in Chicago* (Chicago: University of Chicago Press, 1931); Gerald Suttles, *The Social Order of the Slum* (Chicago: University of Chicago Press, 1968); William Julius Wilson, *The Truly Disadvantaged* (Chicago: University of Chicago Press, 1987). For the best historical treatment of the Chicago school, see Martin Bulmer, *The Chicago School of Sociology: Institutionalization, Diversity, and the Rise of Sociological Research* (Chicago: University of Chicago Press, 1984).

5. Richard Wright, Introduction to St. Clair Drake and Horace Cayton, *Black Metropolis,* pp. xvii–xviii.

6. I have not hidden the identity of this locale for a variety of reasons. First, Valois is a landmark restaurant on the South Side of Chicago that has been written about in numerous newspaper articles. See, for example, "See Your Food," *Reader,* July 24, 1987, and "Count on 50 Year Old Valois for Good Food," *Chicago Tribune,* July 31, 1987.

Because these periodicals have circulations far larger than the number of persons likely to read this book, Valois is already in the widest possible public domain. In addition, my attempts to disguise Valois will only fool those least likely ever to disturb the environment of the cafeteria, readers residing far away who are unfamiliar with the Hyde Park area. Anyone familiar with the South Side is less likely to be fooled by any deceptive efforts on my part. Similarly, while I have disguised the names of most of my subjects to maintain their anonymity, I have used the names of the Greek owners since they have been featured in many articles about the restaurant. See J. Anthony Lukas, "The Fire This Time," *American Prospect*, Spring 1991, pp. 102–13.

7. In this way it is not unlike Junior's Restaurant in Brooklyn, which rightfully proclaims itself "the heart and pulse of downtown Brooklyn." See Nelson George, "On the Menu," *Village Voice*, August 21, 1990, p. 26.

8. For those interested in more detail, Clark went on to say that it was "at Fifty-fifth and Harper, when there were stores there. It was the second store from the corner. A regular restaurant with waitresses. Then, about 1930, he bought this guy out on Lake Park, just a block from where the restaurant stands right now."

9. Sandy Glassman, "Slight Population Changes, Racial Shift Show in New Census Data," *Hyde Park Herald*, April 24, 1991, p. 1.

10. A typical hangout is described in Anderson, *A Place on the Corner*.

11. Robert E. Park, Introduction to Charles S. Johnson, *Shadow of the Plantation* (Chicago: University of Chicago Press, 1934), pp. xi–xiv.

12. See Ralph Ellison, *Shadow and Act* (New York: Vintage Books, 1972).

13. Drake and Cayton, *Black Metropolis*, p. 379. See also Lorraine Hansberry, *To Be Young, Gifted, and Black* (Englewood Cliffs, N.J.: Prentice-Hall, 1969), p. 19. "And sometimes, when Chicago nights got too steamy, the whole family got in the car and went to the park and slept out in the open on blankets."

14. For literature describing life in the ghetto, including particular references to hangouts such as barbershops, see William H. Jones, *Recreation and Amusement among Negroes in Washington, D.C.* (Washington, D.C.: Howard University Press, 1927); Claude McKay, *Harlem: Negro Metropolis* (New York: Dutton, 1940); Drake and Cay-

ton, *Black Metropolis;* Claude Brown, *Manchild in the Promised Land* (New York: Macmillan, 1965); Ulf Hannerz, *Soulside* (New York: Columbia University Press, 1969).

Chapter 4

1. Compare such an attitude with that expressed by the black comedian Eddie Murphy, in a serious interview: "Dr. King has always been a hero of mine. I couldn't be a pacifist the way he was. If somebody calls me a Nigger or gets up in my shit, I'll hit him. I'm a man. You don't pull that shit on me. I'm not with that 'turn the other cheek.'" Elvis Mitchell, "The Prince of Paramount: Eddie Murphy," *Interview* 17, no. 9 (September, 1987).

2. This is a particular example of the more general phenomenon referred to in C. Wright Mills, *The Sociological Imagination* (New York: Oxford University Press, 1959), pp. 3–4. "Yet men do not usually define the troubles they endure in terms of historical change and institutional contradiction. The well-being they enjoy, they do not usually impute to the big ups and downs of the societies in which they live. . . . They cannot cope with their personal troubles in such a way as to control the structural transformations that usually lie behind them."

3. See, for example, Leanita McClain, "The Racial Truth of Politics," *Chicago Tribune,* November 29, 1982: "Whites must stop thinking that *every* black teenager who whisks by on the sidewalk is a thug."

4. Jason DeParle, "Talk of Government Being Out to Get Blacks Falls on More Attentive Ears," *New York Times,* October 29, 1990, Sec. B, p. 7.

5. For a comparison, see Herbert Gans, *The Urban Villagers* (Glencoe: Free Press, 1962), pp. 136–41.

6. For an excellent analysis of the way that black and white cultural differences often cause communication to fail, see Thomas Kochman, *Black and White Styles in Conflict* (Chicago: University of Chicago Press, 1981).

7. Norman H. Nie, Sidney Verba, and John R. Petrocik, *The Changing American Voter* (Cambridge, Mass.: Harvard University Press, 1979), p. 226.

8. For a comparison, see the portrait of white ethnic reactions to

"territorial" and "cultural" threats in Jonathan Rieder, *Canarsie: The Jews and Italians of Brooklyn against Liberalism* (Cambridge, Mass.: Harvard University Press, 1985).

Chapter 5

1. Anderson, *A Place on the Corner,* pp. 40–53.
2. See Jonathan Rubinstein, *City Police* (New York: Farrar, Straus & Giroux, 1973).

Chapter 6

1. Information about the cafeteria during the late seventies is derived from discussions with the Greek owners and local residents.
2. For a relevant study, see Charles Moskos, *Greek Americans* (Englewood Cliffs, N.J.: Prentice-Hall, 1980).
3. George Herbert Mead has referred to the attitude of a whole community as "the generalized other." In many situations, the self-conscious human being assumes or takes the organized social attitudes of the given social group in which he is immersed. See George Herbert Mead, *On Social Psychology,* Selected Papers, edited and with a revised Introduction by Anselm Strauss (Chicago: University of Chicago Press, 1977); see also Erving Goffman, *Behavior in Public Places* (New York: Free Press, 1963).

Chapter 7

1. See the discussion of the nature of exaltation in Rudolf Otto, *Mysticism East and West* (New York: Macmillan Publishing Co., 1932), esp. p. 119.
2. For a general discussion, see Max Weber, *Economy and Society* (Berkeley and Los Angeles: University of California Press, 1979), pp. 1111–58.
3. See Leanita McClain, "How Chicago Taught Me to Hate Whites," *Washington Post,* July 24, 1983.
4. For a theoretical discussion, see Georg Simmel, "The Sociology of Sociability," *American Journal of Sociology* 55, no. 3 (1949).

Chapter 8

1. "Black in White America," ABC News Special, August 29, 1989.

2. "Brothers," *Newsweek,* March 23, 1987.

3. This is not to deny that there are some reporters whose stories are more subtle or that the media do not also sometimes emphasize a population of very worthy people who engage in activities such as organizing residents of housing projects, fighting drug dealers, bringing about other miracles. But my own careful, if unscientific, examination suggests that these are the exceptions rather than the rule.

4. For an impassioned statement, see Bob Blauner, *Black Lives, White Lives* (Berkeley and Los Angeles: University of California Press, 1989), p. 323.

5. Wilson, *The Truly Disadvantaged,* p. 56.

6. See, for example, the papers in Christopher Jencks and Paul Peterson, eds., *The Urban Underclass* (Washington, D.C.: Brookings Institution, 1991).

7. One of the few articles on this subject published during this period is Susan E. Mayer and Christopher Jencks, "Growing Up in Poor Neighborhoods: How Much Does it Matter?" *Science,* 17 March 1989, p. 1441. After summarizing the best available data, the authors conclude, "On the basis of what we now know, we hazard two tentative hypotheses . . . . : 1) When neighbors set social standards for one another or create institutions that serve the entire neighborhood, affluent neighbors are an advantage. 2) When neighbors compete with one another for a scarce resource, such as social standing, good high school grades, or teen age jobs, affluent neighbors are a disadvantage. Because the balance between these two kinds of influence varies from one outcome to another, there is no general rule dictating that affluent neighbors will always been an advantage or a disadvantage."

8. Christopher Jencks, "Is the American Underclass Growing?"

9. Personal Communication, May 3, 1991.

10. *Los Angeles Times,* November 16, 1990, p. C1.

11. In accordance with a longstanding sociological practice of disguising the name of the subject city, Anderson calls the context of his study Eastern City, though it was easily recognized by reviewers as Philadelphia. For an interesting article on the subject of disguising a city in a study of this kind, which influenced my own decisions on

these matters, see J. Anthony Lukas, "The Fire This Time," *American Prospect*, Spring 1991, pp. 102–13.

12. W. E. B. DuBois, *The Philadelphia Negro* (New York: Schocken Books 1967 [first published 1899]), p. 317. Sociologists might still reasonably assert that anecdotal evidence of positive inter-class relationships in black communities can be validated.

13. See also Reynolds Farley, "Residential Segregation of Social and Economic Groups among Blacks, 1970–80," in Christopher Jencks and Paul Peterson, eds., *The Urban Underclass* (Washington, D.C.: Brookings Institution 1991), p. 292.

14. Some of the few studies which conceptualize role models in a more constructive manner are Susan E. Mayer and Christopher Jencks, "Growing Up in Poor Neighborhoods: How Much Does It Matter?" and Susan E. Mayer, "How Much Does a High School's Racial and Socioeconomic Mix Affect Graduation and Teenage Fertility Rates?" (pp. 321–41), James E. Rosenbaum and Susan Popkin, "Employment and Earnings of Low-Income Blacks Who Move to Middle Class Suburbs" (pp. 342–56), Jeffrey M. Berry, Kent E. Portney, and Ken Thomson, "The Political Behavior of Poor People" (pp. 357–74), all in Jencks and Peterson, *The Urban Underclass*.

15. Edward Shils, "Charisma, Order, and Status," in *Center and Periphery* (Chicago: University of Chicago Press, 1975), pp. 256–75.

16. As effective remedies enable more blacks to participate in the mainstream of American life, this social structure will likely appear even more legitimate to members of this population. When progress is turned back, what might otherwise be conceptualized as the legitimate authority of society is more likely conceived as illegitimate domination.

17. Robert K. Merton, *Social Theory and Social Structure* (New York: Free Press, 1968), pp. 356–57.

18. Elisabeth Noelle-Neumann, *The Spiral of Silence* (Chicago: University of Chicago Press, 1984), p. 150.

Chapter 9

1. Shelby Steele, *The Content of Our Character* (New York: St. Martin's Press, 1990).

2. Lee Rainwater, on Ulf Hannerz's *Soulside* (New York: Columbia University Press, Paperback Edition, 1971).

3. Michael B. Katz, *The Undeserving Poor: From the War on Poverty to the War on Welfare* (New York: Pantheon Books, 1989), pp. 170–71.

4. Norman Mailer, "The White Negro: Superficial Reflections on the Hipster," *Advertisements for Myself* (New York: G. P. Putnam's Sons), 1981, p. 341.

5. Charles Keil, *Urban Blues* (Chicago: University of Chicago Press, 1966), p. 8.

6. Elliot Liebow, *Tally's Corner*, p. 59, n. 16.

7. See, for example, Elliot Liebow, *Tally's Corner*, Elijah Anderson, *A Place on the Corner* and *Streetwise*, pp. 69–70. Liebow's work focuses on a group of relatively young men who are members of the black lower class. (Today they might be classified as members of the underclass.) My effort is not to correct him so much as to present an image of the black male which I believe has been underrepresented in sociological studies. Anderson's account in *A Place on the Corner* (and reinforced in *Streetwise*) focuses in part upon the same type of population that I studied, and our findings conflict, for reasons elaborated in note 11.

8. Ralph Ellison, *Shadow and Act* (New York: Random House, 1953), p. 26.

9. Elisabeth Noelle-Neumann, *The Spiral of Silence*, p. 144.

10. For representative essays, see Herbert Blumer, *Symbolic Interactionism: Perspective and Method* (Berkeley: University of California Press, 1986), Howard S. Becker, *Outsiders* (New York: Free Press, 1963), and Erving Goffman, *The Presentation of Self in Everyday Life* (New York: Doubleday, 1959).

11. In these pages I am attempting to provide a corrective for this tendency. Thus whereas I lay stress on the importance of external rewards in understanding the significance of membership in society, I also focus on the internal virtues and strengths of these men in examining their conduct as members of the wider society. For a relevant theoretical statement that is an alternative to Blumer but has not influenced the ethnographers, see Manfred Kuhn, "Major Trends in Symbolic Interaction Theory in the Past Twenty-Five Years," *Sociological Quarterly* 5 (Winter, 1964), pp. 61–84. Theorists must be mindful of the nature of institutional arrangements so that sociological analysis has a solid organizational core and does not deal solely with mechanisms of adjustment. Neither the Kuhn nor the Blumer ap-

proach is appropriate in all situations; one theory or the other will sometimes be particularly fitting in a given setting.

Discrepancies between this account and those of previous scholars derive also from specific differences in social class, ages, and contexts in which the behavior being studied occurred. Thus no generalization about human nature substitutes for a reminder that the black community, and black men in particular, constitute a diverse group. Progress in our conceptions will occur, not by replacing one particular stereotype with another, but rather by eliminating the notion that any generalization will suffice for a category so diverse, embedded in so many diverse situations. Accounts influenced by the theoretical perspective of George Herbert Mead would do better, however, to attempt to discover a particular relationship between internal strength and external honors.

12. Wilson, *The Truly Disadvantaged*, p. 6.

13. Nicholas Lemann, "The Origins of the Underclass," *Atlantic Monthly*, June, 1986, p. 31.

14. *The Promised Land* (New York: Alfred A. Knopf, 1991), p. 348.

15. For an exchange on this subject, see Mitchell Duneier, "Black Migrants Have Done Better," *New York Times*, June 11, 1991. For Lemann's response, see "How to Read the Black Migration to the North," *New York Times*, June 27, 1991. For the most detailed analysis of the problems with Lemann's book, see David Whitman, "The Great Sharecropper Success Story," *Public Interest*, no. 104 (Summer 1991), pp. 3–19, and for the subsequent exchange between Whitman and Lemann, see *Public Interest*, no. 105 (Fall 1991).

16. Lemann, "How to Read the Black Migration to the North."

Chapter 10

1. Martin Kilson and Clement Cottingham, "Thinking about Race Relations: How Far Are We Still from Integration?" *Dissent*, Fall 1991, pp. 520–30.

2. *The Spiral of Silence*, p. 10.

3. For a discussion of this aspect of Hannerz's *Soulside*, see Gerald Suttles, "Urban Ethnography: Situational and Normative Accounts," *Annual Review of Sociology*, p. 12.

4. See, for example, Suttles, *The Social Order of the Slum*, and Anderson, *A Place on the Corner*.

5. Christopher Jencks, *Rethinking Social Policy.*

6. Robert Bly, *Iron John: A Book about Men* (New York: Addison Wesley, 1990.)

7. Robert Bly, "What Men Really Want," in Keith Thompson, ed., *To Be a Man: In Search of the Deep Masculine* (Los Angeles: Jeremy P. Tarcher, 1991), pp. 16–23.

8. This is the phrase Bly uses in discussing today's "soft male."

Index

A

ABC News, "Black in White America," 121–22, 181
Ali, Muhammad, 51, 101
Allman, Walter 52
Anderson, Elijah, 125, 126, 128, 138, 139, 146, 180, 181; on civil rights and culturally nationalist movements, 145; and "no counts," 139; and "old heads," 128; *A Place on the Corner*, 138, 139, 146, 177, 178, 183, 184; on pseudo-kinship tie, 175; *Streetwise*, 125, 128, 129, 138, 175, 183
Atlantic, the, 151, 152, 154
Authority: conflict among various bases of, in ghetto, 131–33; exercising roles, 132; of society, and charisma, 131–32; traditional, 131

B

Bane, Mary Jo, 173
Becker, Howard S., 148, 149, 183
Beliefs of black regulars concerning: affirmative action, 82–83; book learning, 31, 81; child abuse, 73; child rearing and discipline, 71, 72, 73; common sense, 81; conspiracies, 75; degenerate society, AIDS, and drugs, 75; democracy, 71, 73, 74; dependency, 71–72, 125; dominating a relationship, 44–45; experience, 66, 69, 81; foreign policy, 83; genocide, 75, 122; Iran, 82; Iran-Contra affair, 81; Iraq war, 75; manpower vs. computers, 70; reverse discrimination, 82; stock market crash of 1987, 68; "street intelligence," 31; wastefulness, 68, 69; War on Poverty, 83; welfare, 71–72, 125; whites and blacks compared, 44; World Series, 74. *See also* Johnson, Lyndon; King; Reagan
Black class structure, 124, 129
Black identity, 122; disavowal of, 158; definition of, 158, 161
Black males, 166; moral constitution of, 20; under control of criminal justice system, 25; and statistics regarding life chances, 25–26; sociology's typical portrait of, 31; prevailing stereotypes, 40; Elliot Liebow and, 41; as "lovers and

Index